The French Song Anthology

High Voice

Edited by Carol Kimball & Richard Walters

Joel K. Boyd, assistant editor

also available
Accompaniments for the French Song Anthology, High Voice HL00000453

Cover painting: Monet, *The Tuileries*, 1876

ISBN 0-634-03079-5

HAL•LEONARD®
CORPORATION
7777 W. BLUEMOUND RD. P.O. BOX 13819 MILWAUKEE, WI 53213

Visit Hal Leonard Online at
www.halleonard.com

Contents

Preface

"In the art of music, it is the interpreter's performance which we come to regard as the work itself."

—Pierre Bernac

Clarity, elegance, and subtlety are all defining qualities of French music, and nowhere are they more important than in French song. Classical French song, or mélodie, has been called a combination of lyricism and precision, based on the art of suggestion. Good examples are the songs of Gabriel Fauré, in which he creates the atmosphere of the poem by cocooning it in a musical setting of subtly drawn emotions and delicate descriptive moods, devoid of overt details. Does the graceful restraint inherent in the French style render mélodie bloodless and lacking in emotional power? Far from it. Distinguished French baritone Gérard Souzay describes the difference between French and German music this way: "I think that German music kisses you on the forehead and French music on the neck. French music is more sensual—much more sensual—and it is not physical sensuality, it is aesthetic sensuality…French music, like all French art, whether Impressionist or otherwise, wishes to please . . . "

Between 1870 and 1925, Paris emerged as the musical capital of Europe. A specifically French musical nationalism also developed during this period. As the arts developed and flourished, lines of demarcation between them blurred; poets, musicians, and visual artists interconnected in creative projects and social affairs (the notes in this anthology chronicle some of those relationships). During this period French song developed and defined itself. The years spanning the turn of the century (1885-1914) were called *La Belle Époque* (the beautiful age). It was a time of peace, prosperity and artistic ferment in Paris. The city had been redefined geographically by Baron Haussmann into a geometrical grid of avenues and boulevards. Paris was like a large stage, parading its social conventions, taste and fashions for the world to see. Art Nouveau decorated buildings and métro entrances. The music hall and café-concerts became wildly popular venues, spin-offs from the craze for light-opera that Jacques Offenbach had made popular. As the twentieth century appeared, non-Western music from the Great Expositions provided composers with new sources of melody and rhythm, and art and literature also adopted elements from the Orient.

During this explosion of the arts, the mélodie came into its own on Paris' most exclusive stages —the salons. Salons were private gatherings and concerts hosted in the homes of well-to-do patrons of the arts. Salons were places to meet prominent poets, artists, musicians, and novelists of the day. Musical and theatrical performances were spotlighted in the salons. Mélodies were written principally for performance in these settings. Singers were talented amateurs or professionals. Composers often accompanied singers in these performances. Mélodies were also heard at concerts in small halls that retained the intimacy demanded by the form.

The composers included in this volume wrote songs that provide a perspective from which to view the development of French song, and perhaps also, the development of French musical style. Massenet, Gounod, and Bizet are better known for their operas, yet Gounod is termed "the father of the mélodie" and wrote a prolific number of songs. Duparc penned only sixteen songs we know of, but is considered a master of the form. Fauré's songs, numbering more than 100, constantly evolved in style, extending the musical parameters of the genre. Fauré, Duparc and Debussy perfected the mélodie as a true art song form. Franck's influence as a teacher overshadowed his music, but several of his songs are considered classics. Chausson, a Franck disciple, enjoyed working in small forms, and his mélodies contain some exquisite examples of the genre. Possibly the composer most attuned to blending poetry and music was Debussy. Satie's song catalog is quite slim, but his musical style and thought had far-reaching influence. In the twentieth century, Poulenc's fascination with the voice produced 150 mélodies of lasting importance.

The most important forerunner of the mélodie was the *romance*, a simple strophic song form from the eighteenth century. It featured a tuneful vocal line with a modest piano accompaniment (see Martini). By the middle of the nineteenth century, the popularity of the *romance* was waning. Publication and circulation of Schubert's Lieder in France from 1833 on spawned an awareness of the possibilities of merging poetry and music as a strong artistic statement. Midway in the nineteenth century, new romantic poetry by Théophile Gautier, Victor Hugo, Charles Baudelaire, and the Parnassian poets appeared on the scene. Composers seized upon the new, freer verse for their songs. Text and musical setting gradually acquired a closer blend of style and refinement, culminating in the mélodies of Henri Duparc, Ernest Chausson, Emmanuel Chabrier, and the early songs of Gabriel Fauré. Poet Paul Verlaine, who had followed the Parnassians in their elegant but impassive style, broke away to give free rein to his innate lyricism. His work became the touchstone for nineteenth century mélodie. Verlaine created poetry in which word rhythms and nuances attempted to free themselves from prescribed and confining meters, creating verse with its own unique musicality. Poet Stéphane Mallarmé modeled the continuous flow of his texts on Wagner's music. In the early twentieth century, Guillaume Apollinaire's experiments with poetic images and forms found a musical voice in the mélodies of Francis Poulenc. From the Parnassians through Apollinaire, the freer prosody of the new poetry offered composers material from which they fashioned songs with ever stronger musical synthesis between voice and piano.

Since French poetry was a dominant factor in defining the development of the mélodie, the singer needs to be aware of shaping melodic phrase and varying tone color expressively but naturally, to produce the most distinctive vocalization of tone and word. Jane Bathori (1877-1970) and Claire Croiza (1882-1946), two singers who championed the "mélodie française moderne" and worked closely with its composers, repeatedly stressed the importance of the poetry in their master classes and lectures. For Croiza, the *sound of the text* took a secondary role to the *interpretation of the text:* "Here [in singing mélodies], more often than in the theater, the word becomes an element of choice with the fullness of sound, sense, and the beauty of the syllable—a beauty of which our French language is so marvelously rich." Jane Bathori believed the act of artistic creation was based on shaping the musical material; to her, the coherence, clarity and distinction of musical details had tremendous impact on the work as a whole: "In a mélodie, the text is as important as the music; it is necessary to give the color and expression which will best emphasize it. I am not talking about the necessary musicality, but of style and taste, which must be acquired slowly because it changes with the expression of the words, the era that they reflect, and therein resides the difficulty."

The French language itself is often an intimidating barrier to singers tackling French song for the first time. However, the lack of tonic accent in French makes the French repertoire a rich source of material for developing concepts of legato and shaping musical phrase. French should be thought of as a *bel canto* language—it slides and glides in an unstoppable flow. Singing French demands well-placed vowels and clear, rapid consonants. An effective exercise for discovering word meaning and musical structure is to read the poem aloud. It should be declaimed as the composer set it, with all the musical markings on the page. Working with text in this manner heightens aesthetic awareness of the poetry and sharpens response to word meaning, vowel color, and phrase nuance.

In the greatest of French songs, poetry and music join to create a form in which both arts share significantly and depend equally upon each other. Beauty of line and sensuous enjoyment of sound were hallmarks of Paul Verlaine's poetry, which inspired many of the masterpieces of French vocal literature, notably works by Debussy and Fauré. In *Art poétique* (1885) Verlaine wrote that above all, poetry should be "music." Singers working with French song must make the poems sing.

Editors' note: The songs in this anthology are arranged alphabetically by composer. Original keys have been cited where known. In some cases, publication history has made the original key difficult to determine. For the English translations, in general, a word-by-word approach was used, line by poetic line; however, word order was changed to accommodate differences in French and English language structure.

The following sources were consulted in writing the preface and commentaries for the mélodies:

Jane Bathori, *On the Interpretation of the Mélodies of Claude Debussy,* translated and with an introduction by Linda Laurent (Stuyvesant, NY: Pendragon Press, 1998).

Jane Bathori, R.T.F. 1957. Bathori archives. Bibliothèque Nationale, Paris, France.

Claire Croiza Exposition catalogue. Paris: Bibliothèque Nationale, 1984, no. 95.

Pierre Bernac, *The Interpretation of French Song* (New York. W.W. Norton, 1978).

Elaine Brody, Paris: *The Musical Kaleidoscope 1870-1925* (New York: George Braziller, 1987).

Emmanuel Chabrier. *Mélodies (2 vols.)* Le Pupitre, Collection de musique ancienne publiée sous la direction de François Lesure. Edition par Roger Delage. Musica Gallica (Paris: Heugel).

Margaret Cobb, *The Poetic Debussy* (Boston: Northeastern University Press, 1982).

Victor E. Graham, ed., *Sixteenth-Century French Poetry* (Toronto: University of Toronto Press, 1964).

Reynaldo Hahn, *On Singers and Singing (Du chant),* transl. Léopold Simoneau (Portland: Amadeus Press, 1990).

Graham Johnson, Liner notes to *The Songs of Chausson* (Hyperion Records. The Hyperion French Song Edition. CDA 67321/2).

Graham Johnson and Richard Stokes, *A French Song Companion* (Oxford: Oxford University Press, 2000).

Carol Kimball, Song: *A Guide to Style and Literature* (Seattle: Pst., Inc. 1999).

Louise Labé, *Sonnets.* Introduction and commentaries by Peter Sharratt (Austin: University of Texas Press, 1972).

Gerald Larner, *Maurice Ravel* (London: Phaidon Press, 1996).

Timothy LeVan, *Masters of the French Art Song* (Metuchen, NJ: Scarecrow Press, 1991).

Jean-Michel Nectoux, *Gabriel Fauré: a musical life.* transl. by Roger Nichols (Cambridge: Cambridge University Press, 1991).

Sydney Northcote, *The Songs of Henri Duparc* (London: Dennis Dobson, 1959).

Frits Noske, *French Song from Berlioz to Duparc* (New York: Dover, 1970).

Arbie Orenstein, *Ravel: Man and Musician* (New York: Columbia University Press, 1975).

Francis Poulenc, *Moi et mes amis: Confidences recueillies par Stéphane Audel* (Paris: La Palatine, 1963).

Francis Poulenc, *Diary of my Songs [Journal de mes mélodies].* transl. by Winifred Radford (London: Victor Gollancz, Ltd. 1985).

Marie Claire Rohinsky, editor, *The Singer's Debussy* (New York: Pelion Press, 1987).

Louis Simpson, *Modern Poets of France* (Ashland, OR: Story Line Press, 1998).

Roger Shattuck, *The Banquet Years* (New York: Vintage Books, 1968).

Gérard Souzay, Televised interview, collection "Musica: Musicarchive," *Arte,* French documentary by Christian Labrande (O 1962/1994), produced by Philippe Trufo, broadcast 15 October 1995.

Stephen Moore Whiting, *Satie the Bohemian*: from cabaret to concert hall (New York: Oxford University Press, 1999).

Villanelle
from *Les nuits d'été*

Théophile Gautier
(1811-1872)

Hector Berlioz
(1809-1869)

Composed 1840-41. Song no. 1 of *Les nuits d'été*, a cycle of six songs to poems of Théophile Gautier, from his *Comédie de la mort* (1838). In 1843, Berlioz orchestrated "Absence" (no. 4). He completed the remaining orchestrations in 1856, the year he began composing his opera *Les Troyens*. The theme of the six songs is romantic love and longing, seen in various guises. "Villanelle" and the last song, "L'île inconnue," are light-hearted and extroverted. Between these charming "bookend" mélodies are more intense, passionate songs, including two laments. Gautier dedicated this poem "to Mlle. Wolf, singer at the ducal court of Weimar." Berlioz made slight changes to Gautier's original poem, which was titled "Villanelle rhythmique." Other alterations appear in four lines of the poem; the original words are given here in brackets: Stanza 2: Dit ses [des] vers au rebord du nid/Oh! Viens donc sur ce [le] banc de mousse; Stanza 3: Faisant [Faisons] fuir le lapin caché... Puis chez nous, tout heureux [joyeux], tout aises. Berlioz was the first composer to use the term "mélodie" in connection with his songs.

Villanelle

Quand viendra la saison nouvelle,
Quand auront disparu les froids,
Tous les deux nous irons, ma belle,
Pour cueillir le muguet aux bois;
Sous nos pieds égrenant les perles
Que l'on voit au matin trembler,
Nous irons écouter les merles
        Siffler!

Le printemps est venu, ma belle;
C'est le mois des amants béni,
Et l'oiseau, satinant son aile,
Dit ses vers au rebord du nid.
Oh, viens, donc, sur ce banc de mousse,
Pour parler de nos beaux amours,
Et dis-moi de ta voix si douce:
        Toujours!

Loin, bien loin, égarant nos courses,
Faisant fuir le lapin caché,
Et le daim au miroir des sources
Admirant son grand bois penché;
Puis chez nous, tout heureux, tout aises,
En paniers, en laçant nos doigts,
Revenons, rapportant des fraises
        Des bois!

Villanelle

When the new season comes,
When the cold has disappeared,
We two will go, my sweet
To gather lilies-of-the-valley in the woods;
Our feet scattering the pearls of dew
One sees trembling each morning,
We will go to hear the blackbirds
        Whistling!

Spring has come, my sweet
This is the month that lovers bless,
And the bird, smoothing his wing,
Sings verses on the edge of its nest.
Oh, come then, to this mossy bank,
To speak of our beautiful love,
And say to me, in your sweet voice:
        Forever!

Far, very far we'll stray from our path
Startling the rabbit from its hiding place,
And the deer in the mirror of the springs,
Admiring its great lowered antlers;
Then towards home, happy and content,
Our fingers interlaced for baskets,
We'll return, bringing back wild strawberries
        From the woods!

vel - le, Quand au - ront dis - pa - ru les froids, _____

p decresc.

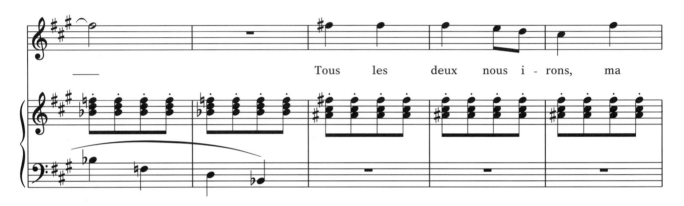

_____ Tous les deux nous i - rons, ma

bel - le, Pour cueil - lir le mu - guet aux bois;

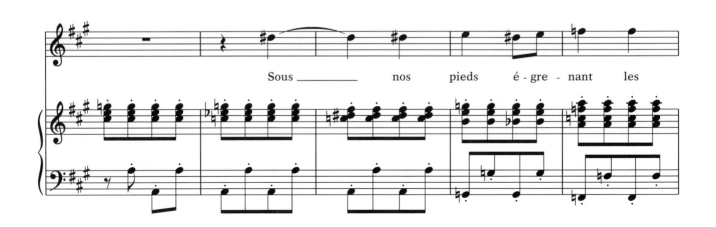

Sous _____ nos pieds é - gre - nant les

per - les Que l'on voit, au ma - tin trem - bler, _____

Nous i - rons é - cou - ter les

mer - les, Nous i - rons é - cou - ter les mer - les, Sif - fler!

Le prin - temps est ve - nu, ma

Loin, bien loin, é-ga-rant nos cour-ses,

Fai - sant fuir le la-pin ca-ché, _____

Et le daim, au mi-roir des sour-ces

sans presser

Ad - mi - rant son grand bois pen - ché;

Puis chez nous, tout heu - reux, tout ai - ses,

En pa - niers, en la - çant nos doigts, _____

Re - ve - nons, rap - por - tant des frai - ses,

Re - ve - nons, rap - por - tant des frai - ses Des bois!

Chanson d'avril

Louis Bouilhet
(1821-1869)

Georges Bizet
(1838-1875)

Composed 1866. No. 1 of Volume 1 (20 songs) published by Choudens (Choudens published 2 volumes of Bizet songs). Here is Bizet at his most melodic, the setting moving squarely in the footsteps of Gounod. Bizet composed 28 mélodies, some of which were published posthumously. His flair for the dramatic and a fine instinct for vocal writing are always predominant qualities of his mélodies.

Chanson d'avril	April Song
Lève-toi! le printemps vient de naître!	Arise! the spring is just born!
Là-bas, sur les vallons, flotte un réseau vermeil!	There, over the valleys floats a rosy veil!
Tout frissonne au jardin, tout chante, et ta fenêtre,	All the garden shivers and sings, and your window,
Comme un regard joyeux, est pleine de soleil!	Like a joyful glance, is full of sunshine!
Du côte des lilas aux touffes violettes,	By the lilacs, purple-clustered,
Mouches et papillons bruissent à la fois	Flies and butterflies hum together
Et le muguet sauvage, ébranlant ses clochettes,	And wild lilies of the valley shaking their tiny bells,
A réveillé l'amour endormi dans les bois!	Have wakened love, sleeping in the woods!
Puisqu'Avril a semé ses marguerites blanches,	Since April has sown her white daisies,
Laisse ta mante lourde et ton manchon frileux;	Put aside your heavy cloak and your cozy muff;
Déjà l'oiseau t'appelle, et tes sœurs les pervenches	Already birds are calling you, and your sisters the periwinkles
Te souriront dans l'herbe en voyant tes yeux bleus!	Will smile in the grass as they see your blue eyes!
Viens, partons! au matin, la source est plus limpide;	Come! Let's go! in the morning the springs are clearer!
Lève-toi ! Viens, partons!	Arise! Come, let's go!
N'attendons pas du jour les brûlantes chaleurs;	Let's not await the burning heat of day;
Je veux mouiller mes pieds dans la rosée humide,	I want to wander with damp feet through the morning dew,
Et te parler d'amour sous les poiriers en fleurs!	And talk to you of love under the flowering pear trees!

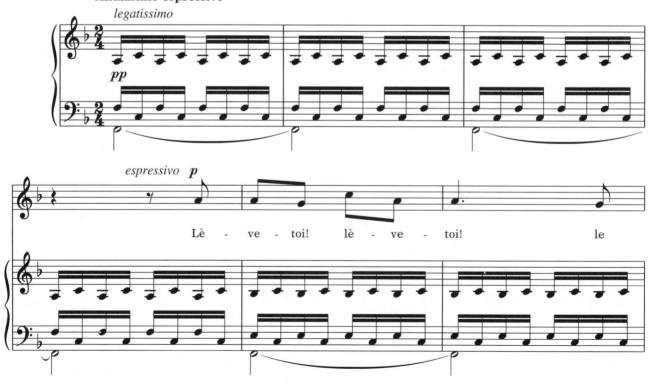

prin - temps vient de naî - tre! Là - bas, sur les val -
lons, flotte un ré - seau ___ ver - meil! ___ Tout
fris - onne au jar - din, tout chante, et ta fe -
nê - tre, Comme un re - gard joy - eux, est plei - ne

fois   Et   le   mu - guet   sau - va - ge, é -

bran - lant   ses   clo - chet - tes,   A   ré - veil -

lé _____ l'a - mour, _____ l'a -

mour   en - dor - mi   dans   les   bois! _____

A ré-veil-lé l'a-mour ____ en-dor-mi ____ dans les bois!

Puisqu'

Av - ril a se - mé ses mar - gue - ri - tes blan - ches, Lais - se ta man - te lourde et ton man - chon ___ fri - leux; ___ Dé - jà l'oi - seau t'ap - pelle, et tes sœurs les per - ven - ches Te

sou - ri - ront dans l'her - be en voy - ant _____ tes yeux

bleus! _____ Viens,

par - tons! au ma - tin, _____ la _____ source est plus lim -

pi - de; Lè - ve— toi! Viens, par - tons! N'at -

cresc.

ten - dons pas du jour les brû - lan - - tes cha -

cresc.

p

leurs; Je veux mouil - ler mes pieds dans

pp

la ro - sée hu - mi - de, Et te _____ par -

crescendo

crescendo

mf

ler _____ d'a - mour, _____ d'a -

mf

Guitare

Victor Hugo
(1802-1885)

Georges Bizet
(1838-1875)

Composed 1866. Song no. 4 of *Feuilles d'Album* (six mélodies to poems of Musset, Ronsard, Hugo, Millevoye and Lamartine). Publisher: Heugel. Bizet composed this mélodie while he was writing his opera *La jolie fille de Perth* (1867). The composer's use of the bolero rhythm animates the song; he referred to it as "exuberant." Bizet added the "Tra-la-las" to the text; they not only lengthen the mélodie, they help underline the uninhibited personality of the protagonist. The leading character of Bizet's masterpiece *Carmen* surely was born from this family tree. Hugo's poem, written in 1838, was titled "Autre guitare," and not "Guitare." A number of other composers set this verse: Victor Massé ("Ramez, dormez, aimez!"), Saint-Saëns ("Guitare"), Liszt ("Comment disaient-ils") and Lalo. Bizet's version is the most famous.

Guitare	Guitar
Comment, disaient-ils,	*Tell us, said the men*
Avec nos nacelles,	*With our small skiffs*
Fuir les alguazils?	*Can we flee from the alguazils?*
—Ramez, disaient-elles.	*—Row, said the fair ones.*
Comment, disaient-ils,	*How, said the men*
Oublier querelles,	*Can we forget quarrels,*
Misère et périls?	*Poverty and danger?*
—Dormez, disaient-elles.	*—Sleep, said the fair ones.*
Comment, disaient-ils,	*How, said the men,*
Enchanter les belles	*Can we enchant beauties*
Sans philtres subtils?	*Without rare potions?*
—Aimez, disaient-elles.	*—Love, said the fair ones.*

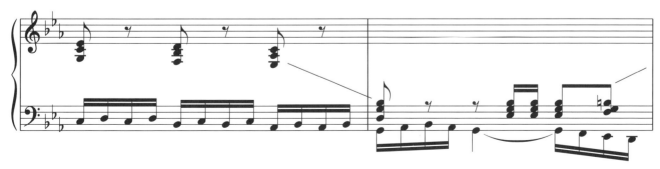

rel - les, Com - ment, di - saient - ils, Ou - bli - er que - rel -

les, Mi - sère et ___ pé - rils? ___

Dor - mez, ___ dor - mez, ___ dor - mez, ___ di - saient -

el - - les. ___

Tra la, la, la, la, la, _____

Com - ment, _ di-saient - ils, _____

Tra, la, la, la, la, la, _____

Ouvre ton cœur

Louis Delâtre
(1815-1893)

Georges Bizet
(1838-1875)

Composed 1859/60. Published by Choudens, volume 2. This song began life as part of a dramatic piece Bizet composed as a student in Rome, the ode-symphony *Vasco de Gama* (1859/60). The work, a composite of opera, oratorio, and symphony, is hardly known today. "Ouvre ton cœur" was published separately and posthumously. It features the bolero rhythm that Bizet was so fond of, and has become a favorite of singers who respond happily to its vocal energy and color. As in "Guitare," this song, with its evocation of Spanish music, also looks forward towards Bizet's opera *Carmen*, especially the "Chanson Bohèmienne" which opens Act 2.

Ouvre ton cœur	*Open your heart*
La marguerite a fermé sa corolle,	*The daisy has closed its flowery crown,*
L'ombre a fermé les yeux du jour.	*Twilight has closed the eyes of day,*
Belle, me tiendras-tu parole?	*My lovely beauty, will you keep your word?*
Ouvre ton cœur à mon amour.	*Open your heart to my love.*
Ouvre ton cœur, ô jeune ange, à ma flamme,	*Open your heart to my desire, young angel*
Qu'en rêve charme ton sommeil.	*May a dream charm your slumber*
Je veux reprendre mon âme,	*I want to take back my soul*
Comme une fleur s'ouvre au soleil!	*As a flower opens to the sun!*

Allegretto

ton — som - meil, Ou - vre ton cœur.

Je — veux

re - pren - dre mon â - me,

Ou - vre ton cœur, ô

Les cigales

Rosemond Gérard
(1866-1953)

Emmanuel Chabrier
(1841-1894)

Composed 1890. Song no. 5 of *Six mélodies*. Published by Enoch, 1890 in two versions, one with "simplified piano accompaniment." The original version is published here. Enoch was afraid Chabrier's difficult accompaniments would discourage amateur pianists and cut back on sales. Chabrier's response: "It seems to me quite useless to redo a few chords here and there; the men or women who sing it will be *musicians*; you cannot claim to be selling it in humble thatched cottages or to be having it sung by adolescents or mere dunderheads . . . " The mélodie is dedicated to Isabelle Jacmart, Chabrier's young niece. Emmanuel Chabrier was the quintessential Gallic personality. His amiable nature is mirrored in his mélodies which infused French song repertoire with wit, whimsy, and good humor (for more information on Chabrier, see "Villanelle des petits canards"). Poetess Rosemond Gérard was eighteen when she met Chabrier. Her first volume of poetry, *Les pipeaux*, had just been published. Among her verses and those of fiancé Edmond Rostand, Chabrier discovered a little bestiary of humorous poems—insightful observations of ducks, turkeys, pigs, and cicadas. He laughingly called these mélodies his "barnyard suite." In setting Gérard's poem, Chabrier made some changes. Her original verse for Stanza 4, verses 3 and 4 was: "Dans les oliviers rabougris/Aux imperceptibles fleurs pâles"; and Stanza 5 read: "Et sur les euphrobes aussi/Agonisant sur la pierraille/C'est encor leur voix qui s'éraille/Dans le pauvre gazon roussi." See the text below for Chabrier's alterations.

Les cigales	The cicadas
Le soleil est droit sur la sente,	The sun is right above the footpath,
L'ombre bleuit sous les figuiers,	The shade turns blue under the fig trees,
Ces cris au loin multipliés,	Those cries, multiplied in the distance
C'est Midi, c'est Midi qui chante!	It is Midday, it's Midday that sings!
Sous l'astre qui conduit le choeur,	Under the star which conducts the chorus,
Les chanteuses dissimulées	The hidden singers
Jettent leurs rauques ululées,	Utter their raucous song
De quel infatigable coeur!	And with what tireless heart!
Le cigales, ces bestioles,	The cicadas, those tiny insects,
Ont plus d'âme que les violes,	Have more soul than the viols,
Les cigales, les cigalons,	The cicadas, the little cicadas,
Chantent mieux que les violons!	Sing better than violins!
S'en donnent elles, les cigales,	They give it their all, the cicadas,
Sur les tas de poussière gris,	On the piles of gray dust,
Sous les oliviers rabougris,	Under the gnarled olive trees
Étoilés de fleurettes pâles.	Starred with pale blossoms.
Et grises de chanter ainsi,	And exhilarated from singing like this,
Elles font leur musique folle;	They make their crazy music,
Et toujours leur chanson s'envole	And still their song soars relentlessly
Des touffes du gazon roussi!	From the tufts of scorched grass!
Le cigales, ces bestioles,	The cicadas, those tiny insects,
Ont plus d'âme que les violes,	Have more soul than the viols,
Les cigales, les cigalons,	The cicadas, the little cicadas,
Chantent mieux que les violons!	Sing better than violins!
Aux rustres épars dans le chaume,	To the peasants scattered in the fields,
Le grand astre torrentiel,	The great burning sun,
A larges flots, du haut du ciel,	Flooding down from the high heavens,
Verse le sommeil et son baume.	Pours sleep and its balm.
Tout est mort, rien ne bruit plus	Everything is dead, there is no sound but theirs
Qu'elles, toujours, les forcenées	Frenzied and incessantly heard
Entre les notes égrénées	Amid the far-flung notes
De quelque lointain angélus!	Of some distant angelus!
Le cigales, ces bestioles,	The cicadas, those tiny insects,
Ont plus d'âme que les violes,	Have more soul than the viols,
Les cigales, les cigalons,	The cicadas, the little cicadas,
Chantent mieux que les violons!	Sing better than violins!

44

Villanelle des petits canards

Rosemond Gérard
(1866-1953)

Emmanuel Chabrier
(1841-1894)

Composed 1890. No. 1 of *Six mélodies*. Published by Enoch, 1890. Dedicated to Mlle. Mily-Meyer. First performance: Paris, 7 March 1890, Théâtre du Vaudeville, by the dedicatée. Chabrier described her as a "light singer—the smallest, the prettiest, the most fragile of operetta stars—she is the Tom Thumb of the theatrical world." Of his "barnyard suite" settings (see "Les cigales") Chabrier wrote: ". . . these songs cannot make it straight off; they are new and disconcerting; at first, only smart people will find them funny, then the others will join in . . . in order for them to please, you must have two artists, one at the piano, the other standing up, and no dullards in the audience. It's a lot to ask for, but it will come in time." Chabrier was as interested in poetry and painting as he was in music, and enjoyed the friendship of some of the most distinguished writers and artists of his day. He collected paintings by Cezanne, Renoir, and Manet long before they were recognized masters. Chabrier's portrait was painted by Manet, Degas, and Fantin-Latour. Rollo Meyers points out that Chabrier is too often dismissed as a minor composer of light music: " . . . it should not be forgotten that he was also a bold innovator who anticipated, in his harmonic language especially, many of the procedures which later became an integral part of the idiom of composers like Debussy and Ravel—both of whom, incidentally, thought very highly of him." Composer Francis Poulenc showed his high regard for Chabrier by writing a biography of the composer: "Ah! Chabrier, I love him as one loves a father! An indulgent father, always merry, his pockets full of tasty tidbits. Chabrier's music is a treasure house you can never exhaust; I just-could-not-do-without-it! It consoles me on my darkest days."

Villanelle des petits canards

Ils vont, les petits canards,
Tout au bord de la rivière,
Comme de bons campagnards!

Barboteurs et frétillards,
Heureux de troubler l'eau claire,
Ils vont, les petits canards,
Ils semblent un peu jobards,
Mais ils sont à leur affaire,
Comme de bons campagnards!

Dans l'eau pleine de têtards,
Où tremble une herbe légère,
Ils vont, les petits canards,
Marchant par groupes épars,
D'une allure régulière,
Comme de bons campagnards!

Dans le beau vert d'épinards
De l'humide cressonnière,
Ils vont, les petits canards,
Et quoiqu'un peu goguenards,
Ils sont d'humeur débonnaire
Comme de bons campagnards!

Faisant, en cercles bavards,
Un vrai bruit de pétaudière,
Ils vont, les petits canards,
Dodus, lustrés et gaillards,
Ils sont gais à leur manière,
Comme de bons campagnards!

Villanelle of the little ducks

They go, the little ducks,
All along the river bank,
Like good countryfolk!

Paddling and waggling their tails,
Happy to muddy the clear water
They go, the little ducks,
They look a little foolish
But they take care of their business,
Like good countryfolk!

In the water full of tadpoles,
Where delicate reeds tremble,
They go, the little ducks,
Marching in scattered groups
At a well-regulated pace,
Like good countryfolk!

In the beautiful spinach-green
Of the moist watercress bed
They go, the little ducks,
And though a little roguish
They are really good-natured,
Like good countryfolk!

Making, in chattering circles,
A really terrible racket,
They go, the little ducks,
Plump, glossy, and merry
They are gay in their own way,
Like good countryfolk!

Allegretto con moto

très simplement et très rythmé

Ils vont, les pe - tits ca - nards, Tout au bord de

la ri - viè - re, Com - me de bons cam - pa - gnards! _____

Bar - bo - teurs et fré - til - lards, Heu - reux de trou - bler l'eau

clai - re, Ils vont, les pe - tits ca - nards, Ils sem - blent un

peu jo - bards, Mais ils sont à leur af - fai - re,

Com - me de bons cam - pa - gnards! _____

Dans l'eau plei - ne de tê - tards, Où

tremble une her - be lé - gè - re, Ils vont, les pe - tits ca - nards,

Mar - chant par grou - pes é - pars, D'une al - lu - re

ré - gu - liè - re, Com - me de bons cam - pa - gnards! ____

Dans le beau vert d'é - pi - nards De l'hu -

Lamento

Théophile Gautier
(1811-1872)

Henri Duparc
(1848-1933)

Composed 1883. Original key: D minor. Published by Rouart-Lerolle, 1911. Dedicated to Gabriel Fauré. The poem, taken from Gautier's *Comédie de la Mort* (1832) was also used by Berlioz in *Les nuits d'été* (titled "Au cimetière"). Duparc used only three stanzas of the original poem's six stanzas. Between stanzas 1 and 2 of the mélodie there is one omitted stanza; between stanzas 2 and 3 there are two omitted stanzas. Gautier's poem is full of repeated vowel sounds (*roucoulement, doucement / l'unison, tombe, l'ombre, colombe*) that call to mind the plaintive cooing sounds of the dove, and perpetuate the melancholy poetic mood. Duparc's somber opening motive is repeated hypnotically throughout the song. The composer's dedication to Fauré is also significant. Duparc might have composed this song in homage; the vocal line shows the suppleness and elegant curve characteristic of Fauré's style, and the overall musical setting is one of studied restraint.

Lamento	Lament
Connaissez-vous la blanche tombe	*Do you know the white tomb*
Où flotte avec un son plaintif	*Where with a plaintive sound, floats*
L'ombre d'un if?	*The shadow of a yew tree?*
Sur l'if une pâle colombe,	*On the yew a pale dove,*
Triste et seule au soleil couchant,	*Sad and alone in the setting sun,*
Chante son chant.	*Sings its song.*
On dirait que l'âme éveillée	*As though the awakened soul*
Pleure sous terre à l'unisson	*Weeps, under the earth, in unison*
De la chanson,	*With the song,*
Et du malheur d'être oubliée	*And from the unhappiness of being forgotten*
Se plaint dans un roucoulement,	*Moans in cooing sounds*
Bien doucement.	*Very softly.*
Ah! jamais plus près de la tombe	*Ah! Nevermore near the tomb*
Je n'irai, quand descend le soir	*Shall I go, when night descends*
Au manteau noir,	*In its black cloak,*
Écouter la pâle colombe	*To hear the pale dove*
Chanter, sur la branche de l'if,	*Sing on the branch of a yew*
Son chant plaintif?	*Its plaintive song.*

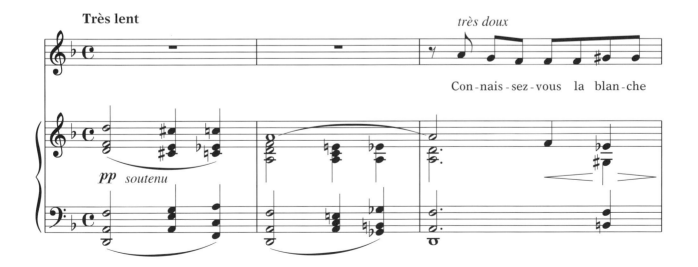

tom - be Où flotte a - vec un son plain - tif L'om - bre d'un if? Sur

l'if u - ne pâ - le co - lom - be, Triste et seule au so-leil cou - chant, Chan - te son

chant. On di-rait que l'âme é-veil -lé - e Pleu-re sous terre ____ à l'u-nis - son De la chan -

son, Et du mal - heur d'ê - tre ou - bli - é - e Se plaint dans un rou-cou-le -

ment, Bien dou - ce - ment.

Un peu plus animé

Ah! ja - mais plus près de la tom - be Je n'i - rai, quand de - scend le soir Au man - teau noir, É - cou -

Chanson triste

Jean Lahor
(1840-1909)

Henri Duparc
(1848-1933)

Composed 1868. Original key: E-flat. Later orchestrated by the composer. Published by Rouart-Lerolle, 1911. Dedicated to M. Leon MacSwiney, Duparc's brother-in-law. MacSwiney was an amateur singer—obviously of considerable skill. Duparc left only sixteen songs, but they are among the most beautiful in the French repertoire. He continually polished and revised his mélodies and often destroyed many he felt were not worthy of publication. Duparc conceived most of his songs for what he called "the violin-voice," capable of fluent, flexible phrasing and real intensity of tone. "Chanson triste" was Duparc's first mélodie. Its slightly sentimental qualities link it to the salon style of Gounod, although Duparc's stylistic fingerprints can also be seen: a rich piano texture of arpeggios that urge the song forward, an expressive bass line, and spacious, flowing vocal phrases. Duparc chose poetry of living poets, all from the Parnassian school. (The Parnassians were a group of French poets were chiefly concerned with the classic ideals of the Greeks. Their poetry is elegant but highly impersonal in style, often containing a colorful orientalism.) Jean Lahor was one of the pen names of Dr. Henri Cazalis, a well-traveled intellectual. He was highly interested in oriental culture and thought, and his Buddhist sympathies earned him the title "Hindou du Parnasse Contemporain." His verses inspired two other Duparc songs: "Extase," and "Sérénade Florentine."

Chanson triste	*Sorrowful Song*
Dans ton cœur dort un clair de lune,	*In your heart sleeps moonlight,*
Un doux clair de lune d'été,	*A soft summer moonlight,*
Et pour fuir la vie importune	*And to escape life's worries,*
Je me noierai dans ta clarté.	*I shall drown myself in your light.*
J'oublierai les douleurs passées,	*I will forget past sorrows,*
Mon amour, quand tu berceras	*My love, when you cradle*
Mon triste cœur et mes pensées,	*My sad heart and my thoughts,*
Dans le calme aimant de tes bras.	*In the loving calm of your arms.*
Tu prendras ma tête malade	*You will take my sick head*
Oh! quelquefois sur tes genoux,	*Oh! sometimes on your knee*
Et lui diras une ballade	*And will tell it a ballad*
Qui semblera parler de nous.	*That will seem to speak of us.*
Et dans tes yeux pleins de tristesses,	*And from your eyes full of sadness*
Dans tes yeux alors je boirai	*From your eyes I shall drink*
Tant de baisers et de tendresses	*So many kisses and so much tenderness*
Que, peut-être, je guérirai…	*That, perhaps, I will heal…*

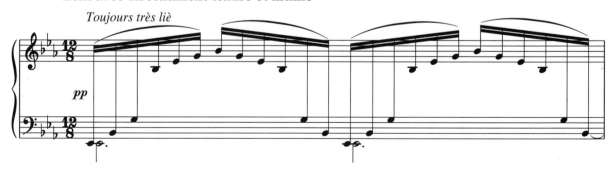

poco più *f* *très doux*

J'ou - blie-rai les dou - leurs pas - sé - es, Mon a - mour,

poco più *f* *p*

quand tu ber - ce - ras Mon tris - te cœur et mes pen - sé - es,

poco cresc.

poco cresc.

Dans le calme ai - mant _____ de tes bras. _____

p *opt.*

p

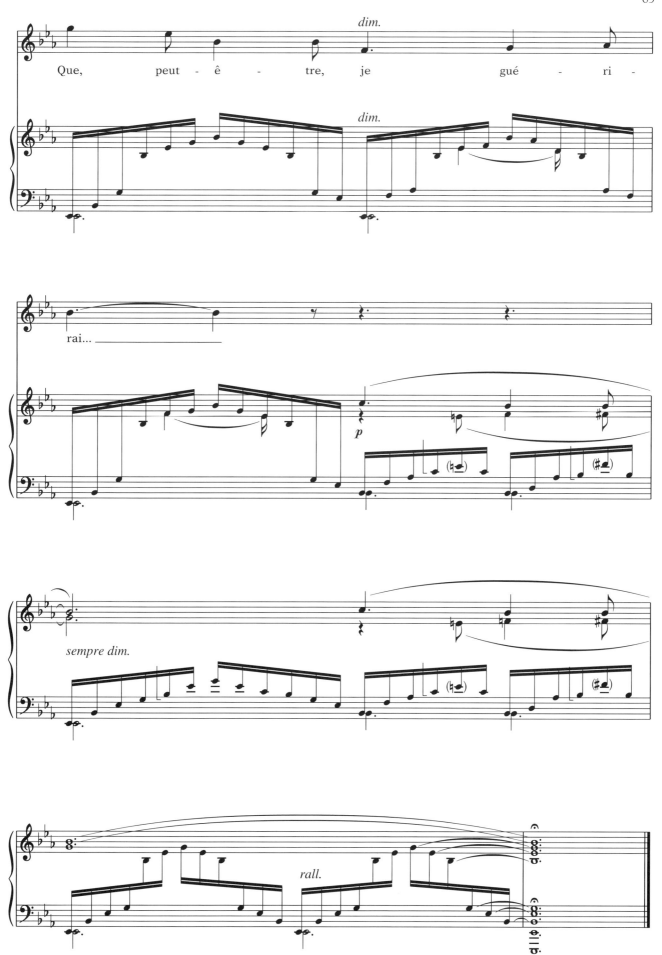

Que, peut - ê - tre, je gué - ri -

rai...

La vie antérieure

Charles Baudelaire
(1821-1867)

Henri Duparc
(1848-1933)

Composed 1884. Originally composed for voice and orchestra. Original key: E-flat major. Dedicated to J. Guy Ropartz. Published by Rouart-Lerolle, 1911. Charles Baudelaire, the greatest of the poets set by Duparc, is often called the "father of modern poetry." A perverse and troubled genius, Baudelaire was drawn to unique, dark themes, and had a predilection for mysticism and ritualistic religion. His intensely personal poems reflect his decadent life style. "La vie antérieure" is extracted from Baudelaire's *Les fleurs du mal* (1857) which created a scandal when it first appeared. The author, publisher, and printer were successfully prosecuted and the book was suppressed because of its alleged immorality. Singer Charles Panzéra (1896-1976) describes this mélodie as "glowing with that strange Baudelairian light—near and far away, captivating and mysterious." Duparc's indication for the last section of the song is "almost half voice, with no nuance, like a vision." In the third stanza, Duparc repeats "C'est là" as if to emphasize the seductive force of that illusion. "La vie antérieure" was Duparc's last mélodie.

La vie antérieure

J'ai longtemps habité sous de vastes portiques
Que les soleils marins teignaient de mille feux,
Et que leurs grands piliers, droits et majestueux,
Rendaient pareils, le soir, aux grottes basaltiques.

Les houles, en roulant les images des cieux,
Mêlaient d'une façon solennelle et mystique
Le tout-puissants accords de leur riche musique
Aux couleurs du couchant reflété par mes yeux.

C'est là que j'ai vécu dans les voluptés calmes,
Au milieu de l'azur, des vagues, des splendeurs
Et des esclaves nus, tout imprégnés d'odeurs,

Qui me rafraîchissaient le front avec des palmes,
Et dont l'unique soin était d'appronfondir
Le secret douloureux qui me faisait languir.

The former life

For a long time I lived under vast porticos
Which the suns of the sea tinted with a thousand fires
And whose great pillars, straight and majestic,
Made them look, at evening, like caves of basalt.

The surging waves, mirroring the image of the skies,
Solemnly and majestically mingled
The all-powerful chords of their rich music
With the colors of the sunset reflected in my eyes.

It is there I lived in calm, sensual pleasure,
Amid azure skies, waves, splendors
And naked slaves, lavishly perfumed,

Who cooled my brow with palm fronds,
And whose only care was to deepen
The sad secret that made me languish.

Lent et solennel

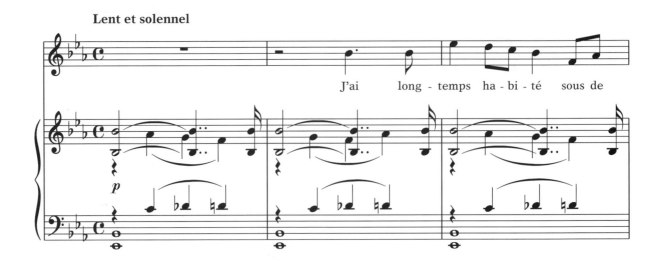

vas - tes por - ti - - ques Que les so - leils ma - rins tei - gnaient de mil - le

feux, Et que leurs grands pi - liers, droits et ma -

jes - tu - eux, Ren - daient pa - reils, le soir, aux

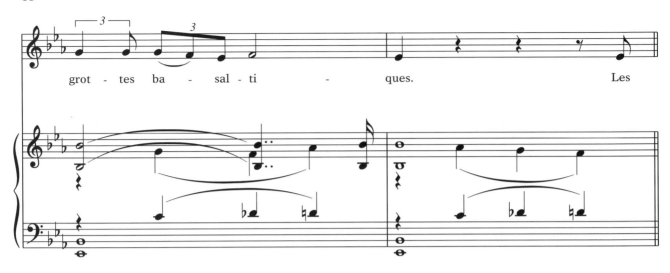

grot - tes ba - sal - ti - ques. Les

Un peu plus vite mais très peu

hou - les, en rou - lant les i - ma - ges des

cieux, _____ Mê - laient d'u - ne fa -

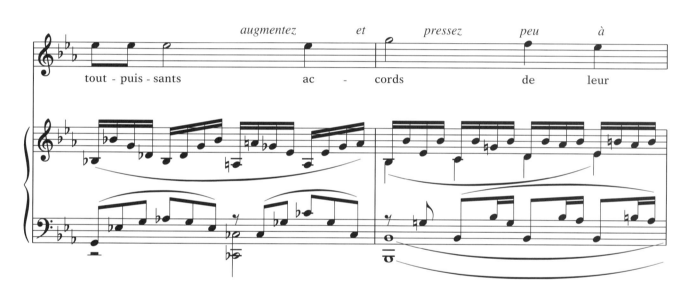

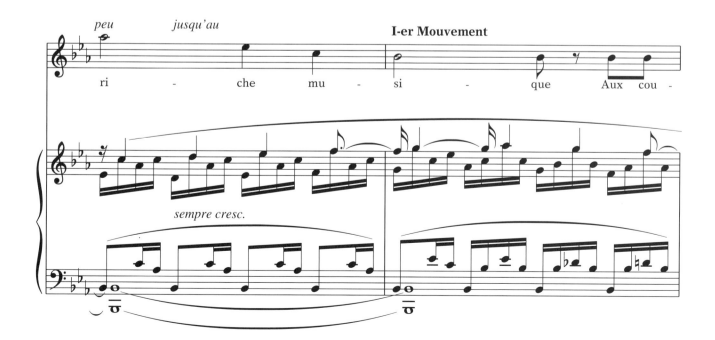

sempre cresc.

leurs   du   cou - chant   re - flé -

augmentez   et   **ff** pressez   toujours

té   par   mes   yeux.

sempre cresc.

10

10

sempre cresc.

reux _____ qui me fai - sait lan - guir.

un peu ralenti

dim.

pp

perdendo

Hébé

Louise Ackermann
(1813-1890)

Ernest Chausson
(1855-1899)

Composed 1882. Opus 2, no. 6, subtitled "Chanson grecque dans le mode phrygien." Publisher: Hamelle. Dedicated to Mlle. Eva Callimaki-Catargi, a young woman probably of Greek origin. She was painted twice by Fantin-Latour. In his painting titled *La leçon de dessin* she is portrayed copying a Greek plaster. Louise Ackermann, née Victorine Choquet, was a late romantic poetess. "Hébé" is found in her collection titled *Contes et poésies* (1863). Chausson was fascinated by eastern religions, especially Buddhism, and his attraction to this volume of poetry might have stemmed from its material on Savitri and Sakuntala. The divine cupbearer of the gods, Hébé, pours the elixir of youth. The poem is austere but elegant in its illustration of the young Grecian goddess; Chausson's use of the Phrygian mode evokes a mood of antiquity. Despite the grandeur of the poetic content, there is a sense of intimacy in the little scene of Hébé and the gods, a microcosm suspended in time, classic and complete.

Hébé

Les yeux baissés, rougissante et candide,
Vers leur banquet, quand Hébé s'avançait,
Les Dieux charmés tendaient leur coupe vide,
Et de nectar l'enfant la remplissait.

Nous tous aussi, quand passe la jeunesse,
Nous lui tendons notre coupe à l'envi.
Quel est le vin qu'y verse la Déesse?
Nous l'ignorons; il enivre et ravit.

Ayant souri dans sa grâce immortelle,
Hébé s'éloigne; on la rappelle en vain.
Longtemps encor, sur la route éternelle,
Notre œil en pleurs suit l'échanson divin.

Hébé

Her eyes lowered, blushing and ingenuous,
When Hébé drew near their banquet
The enchanted Gods held out their empty cups,
And the child refilled them with nectar.

All we too, when youth has passed.
Hold out our cup to her with longing.
What is the wine the Goddess pours there?
We do not know; it intoxicates and delights.

Having smiled in her immortal grace,
Hébé goes on her way; we call her back in vain.
On the eternal path, for a long time still
Our tearful eyes follow the divine cup-bearer.

76

Le charme

Armand Silvestre
(1837-1901)

Ernest Chausson
(1855-1899)

Composed 1879. Op. 2, No. 2. Publisher: Hamelle. Armand Silvestre's poem appears in *Chansons des heures*. The poem is titled "Pour une voix," and is found in the section of poems titled *Vers pour être chanté*. Fauré set "Le plus doux chemin" from this volume. Silvestre was a well-known poet and novelist of the day. His poetry is extricably bound up with the history of French song; Fauré and Massenet used his verses extensively. Silvestre poems were also set by Bizet, Delibes, Duparc, Lalo, and Roussel. "Le charme" is one of the very earliest of Chausson's songs. It has all the simplicity and attractive qualities of a salon song. At the time he composed it, Chausson was studying with Jules Massenet, and had just begun attending the classes of César Franck. Perhaps Massenet's fondness for Silvestre's poetry prompted Chausson's choice of text for this song. It was to be Chausson's only setting of the poet.

Le charme	The Charm
Quand ton sourire me surprit,	*When your smile surprised me*
Je sentis frémir tout mon être,	*I felt all my being tremble*
Mais ce qui domptais mon esprit	*But what had subdued my spirit*
Je ne pus d'abord le connaître.	*At first I could not know.*
Quand ton regard tomba sur moi,	*When your gaze fell upon me*
Je sentis mon âme se fondre,	*I felt my soul melt,*
Mais ce que serait cet émoi,	*But what this emotion might be,*
Je ne pus d'abord en répondre.	*At first I could not understand.*
Ce qui me vainquit à jamais,	*What vanquished me forever*
Ce fut un plus douloureux charme,	*Was a much sadder charm,*
Et je n'ai su que je t'aimais,	*And I did not know that I loved you*
Qu'en voyant ta première larme.	*Until I saw your first tear.*

Le temps des lilas

Maurice Bouchor
(1855-1929)

Ernest Chausson
(1855-1899)

Composed 1886. Publisher: Rouart-Lerolle. This poem is found in Maurice Bouchor's volume *Les poèmes de l'amour et de la mer* (1876) in the section titled "La mort de l'amour." Chausson's setting for voice and piano is probably his most famous mélodie. He later used the song as the third movement of his orchestral song cycle titled *Poème de l'amour et de la mer*, Opus 19. Its memorable opening theme was also the basis for the second movement of that work, the orchestral Interlude. A full score was published in 1919, after the composer's death. Chausson dedicated the *Poème de l'amour et de la mer* to Henri Duparc. The first performance was sung by Désiré Demest in Brussels, 21 February 1893. Maurice Bouchor and Chausson were contemporaries and close friends. Chausson composed a total of eight mélodies to Bouchor's verses during the period from 1878 to 1888. As the century drew to a close, reminiscence became a prominent poetic theme. Bouchor's poem emphasizes loss, change, and nostalgia for things past.

Le temps des lilas	*The time of lilacs*
Le temps des lilas et le temps des roses	*The time of lilacs and the time of roses*
Ne reviendra plus à ce printemps-ci;	*Will not return again this spring*
Le temps des lilas et le temps des roses	*The time of lilacs and the time of roses*
Est passée, le temps des œillets aussi,	*Is passed, the time of carnations too.*
Le vent a changé, les cieux sont moroses,	*The wind has changed, the skies are gloomy,*
Et nous n'irons plus courir, et cueillir	*And we will go no more to gather*
Les lilas en fleur et les belles roses;	*The flowering lilacs and the beautiful roses;*
Le printemps est triste et ne peut fleurir.	*The spring is sad and cannot blossom.*
Oh! joyeux et doux printemps de l'année,	*Oh! joyful and sweet spring of the year,*
Qui vins, l'an passé, nous ensoleiller,	*That came last year to bathe us in sunshine,*
Notre fleur d'amour est si bien fanée,	*Our flower of love is now so withered*
Las que ton baiser ne peut l'éveiller!	*Alas! your kiss cannot revive it!*
Et toi, que fais-tu? pas de fleurs écloses,	*And you, what are you doing? No budding flowers,*
Point de gai soleil ni d'ombrages frais;	*No cheerful sunlight or cool shadows*
Le temps des lilas et le temps des roses	*The time of lilacs and the time of roses*
Avec notre amour est mort à jamais.	*With our love, is dead forever.*

Le temps des li - las _____ et le temps des ro - ses _____

Ne re-vien-dra plus _____ à ce prin-temps -ci; _____

Le temps des li - las _____ et le temps des ro - ses Est pas - sée, _____

_____ le temps des œil-lets aus - si, _____

Le colibri

Leconte de Lisle
(1818-1894)

Ernest Chausson
(1855-1899)

Composed 1882. Opus 2, no. 7. Publisher: Hamelle. Dedicated to Lady Harbord. The seven songs of Opus 2 ("Nanny," "Le charme," "Les papillons," "Le dernière feuille," "Sérénade italienne," "Hébé," and " Le colibri") contain a variety of subject matter, but are especially notable for their effective synthesis of music and poetry. Chausson was particularly attracted to the poetry of Charles Marie René Leconte (known as de Lisle because of his birthplace), the leader of the Parnassian poets. The Parnassians stressed restraint, objectivity, and precise description in their poetry. De Lisle's verse is rich in imagery, color, rhythm, and veiled sensuality. Chausson's setting is full of subtle nuance; even the unusual metric signature (5/4) seems natural. The sultry world of the hummingbird could easily be linked to the paintings of Paul Gauguin, a friend of Chausson. Chausson's superb personal collection of paintings included not only canvasses by Gauguin, but also Delacroix, Corot, Renoir, Degas, and Japanese prints by the great masters. It is little wonder that Chausson was drawn to de Lisle's poetic images.

Le colibri	The hummingbird
Le vert colibri, le roi des collines,	The green hummingbird, the king of the hills,
Voyant la rosée et le soleil clair	Seeing the dew and the bright sunlight
Luire dans son nid tissé d'herbes fines,	Shining on his nest woven from fine grasses
Comme un frais rayon s'échappe dans l'air.	Like a fresh ray, escapes into the air.
Il se hâte et vole aux sources voisines,	He hurries and flies to the nearby springs
Où les bambous font le bruit de la mer,	Where bamboos make a sound like the sea
Où l'açoka rouge, aux odeurs divines,	Where the divinely perfumed red hibiscus
S'ouvre et porte au cœur un humide éclair.	Unfolds the dewy brilliance of its heart.
Vers la fleur dorée il descend, se pose,	To the gilded flower he descends, he hovers
Et boit tant d'amour dans la coupe rose	And drinks so much love from the red cup
Qu'il meurt, ne sachant s'il l'a pu tarir.	That he dies, not knowing if he has drained it!
Sur la lèvre pure, ô ma bien-aimée,	On your pure lips, o my beloved
Telle aussi mon âme eût voulu mourir	My soul would also have wished to die
Du premier baiser qui l'a parfumée!	Of the first kiss which perfumed it!

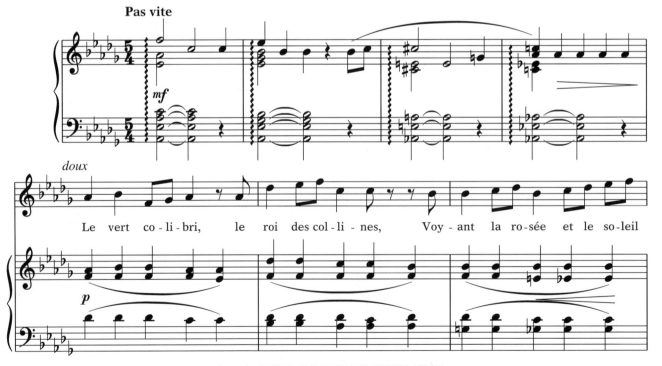

clair Lui-re dans son nid tis - sé d'her-bes fi - nes, ___

Comme un frais ra - yon s'é-chap-pe dans l'air. ___

Il se hâte ___ et vole aux sour-ces voi - si - nes, ___

en pressant peu à peu

Où les bam-bous font le bruit de la mer, ___

en pressant peu à peu

Beau soir

Paul Bourget
(1852-1935)

Claude Debussy
(1862-1918)

Some sources date this song 1877/78; however Rohinsky dates it 1882, and Cobb suggests 1883 as a likely year for its composition. Bourget's poem is found in *Les Aveux II*, first published in 1882; "En voyage", no. VII, in *Dilettantisme*. Published by Vve E. Girod 1891; Fromont, 1919; Jobert, n.d. Arranged for violin and piano by A. Bachmann (Jobert, 1909); for orchestra by H. Mouton (Jobert, 1926); and for cello and piano (Jobert, 1923). Debussy composed "Beau soir" at twenty or twenty-one years of age, and before his journey to Rome in 1884 as winner of the Prix de Rome. It was not published until 1891, the year before the premiere of *Pelléas et Mélisande*. It is difficult to recognize much of Debussy's characteristic musical style in this early mélodie. He does, however, tip his cap to Massenet with supple, graceful vocal phrases. See "Les cloches" for information on Bourget.

Beau soir

Lorque au soleil couchant les rivières sont roses,
Et qu'un tiède frisson court sur les champs de blé,
Un conseil d'être heureux semble sortir des choses
Et monter vers le cœur troublé.

Un conseil de goûter le charme d'être au monde
Cependant qu'on est jeune et que le soir est beau,
Car nous nous en allons, comme s'en va cette onde:
Elle à la mer, nous au tombeau.

Beautiful evening

When at sunset the rivers are rose-tinted
And a warm breeze shivers across the wheat fields,
A suggestion to be happy seems to emanate from all things
And rises towards the restless heart.

A suggestion to savor the pleasure of being alive
While one is young and the evening is beautiful
For we shall go, as this waves goes:
It to the sea, we to the tomb.

93

poco rit. *a tempo* *p*

blé.

Un con - seil de goû - ter le

char - me d'être au mon - de

animato poco a poco e cresc.

Ce - pen - dant qu'on est jeune et que le soir est

f *dim.*

beau, _____ Car nous nous en al -

Les cloches

Paul Bourget
(1852-1935)

Claude Debussy
(1862-1918)

Composed 1891? No. 2 *Deux romances* (No. 1 is "Romance"). Publisher: Durand, 1891. The style of *Deux romances* suggests the two songs were probably composed well before publication; Cobb suggests the date 1886. The text is taken from Bourget's *Dilettantisme*, in *Les Aveux II*, 1882. The title of Bourget's poem is "Romance." The song manuscript is untitled; the publisher added the title "Les cloches." Paul Bourget, critic and novelist noted for his intellect, was a poet associated with a number of Debussy's early songs. Debussy's settings of Bourget's verses are lyrical and nostalgic (see "Beau soir"), and are musically linked to early Fauré or Massenet in style.

Les cloches

Les feuilles s'ouvraient sur le bord des branches,
    Délicatement,
Les cloches tintaient, légères et franches,
    Dans le ciel clément.

Rythmique et fervent comme une antienne,
    Ce lointain appel
Me remémorait la blancheur chrétienne
    Des fleurs de l'autel.

Ces cloches parlaient d'heureuses années,
    Et dans le grand bois,
Semblaient reverdir les feuilles fanées
    Des jours d'autrefois.

The bells

The leaves opened on the edges of the branches,
    Delicately,
The bells pealed, light and clear,
    In the mild sky.

Rhythmic and fervent like an anthem,
    That distant peal
Brought to mind the Christian whiteness
    Of altar flowers.

Those bells spoke of happy years,
    And in the great woods,
Seemed to turn green again the faded leaves
    Of days gone by.

Mandoline

Paul Verlaine
(1844-1896)

Claude Debussy
(1862-1918)

Composed 1882. Song no. 3 in the *Vasnier Songbook*. Publisher, *La Revue illustrée*, September 1, 1890, with illustrations by Willette; Durand et Schoenewerk, Paris, 1890; Durand 1905, 1907. Arranged for voice and orchestra by Louis Beydts; Durand, 1930. There are two manuscripts: a dated manuscript with the dedication in the Bibliothèque Nationale, Paris, and an undated manuscript in the Houghton Library, Harvard University. There are text changes in the undated manuscript: C'est Tircis et c'est *Lycandre* (Debussy)/ C 'est Tircis et c'est *Aminte* (Verlaine); D'une lune *grise et rose* (Debussy)/ D'une lune *rose et grise* (Verlaine). On the back of the last page of this manuscript are found the first sixteen bars of an early version of "En sourdine," without the words. "Mandoline" is dedicated to Mme. Vasnier ("These songs that lived only through her and that would lose their charming grace were they nevermore to issue from her melodious fairy mouth, the author eternally grateful.") Marie-Blanche Vasnier was a gifted amateur singer with whom the young Debussy was infatuated. Debussy composed a volume of thirteen songs, the so-called "Vasnier Songbook," as a gift for her. Their tumultuous liaison ended around 1887. Debussy was the first composer of importance to set Verlaine's poetry. Fauré, Hahn, Chabrier, Milhaud, Ravel, Chausson, and others followed him. (See Fauré's "Mandoline", composed eight years later).

Mandoline	*Mandolin*
Les donneurs de sérénades	*The serenaders*
Et les belles écouteuses,	*And their lovely listeners,*
Échangent des propos fades	*Exchange trivial banter*
Sous les ramures chanteuses.	*Under the singing boughs.*
C'est Tircis et c'est Aminte,	*It is Tircis and Aminte,*
Et c'est l'éternel Clitandre,	*And the tiresome Clitandre,*
Et c'est Damis qui pour mainte	*And Damis, who for many a*
Cruelle fait maint vers tendre.	*Cruel woman writes many a tender verse.*
Leurs courtes vestes de soie,	*Their short silken jackets,*
Leurs longues robes à queues,	*Their long dresses with trains*
Leur élégance, leur joie,	*Their elegance, their merriment,*
Et leurs molles ombres bleues,	*And their soft blue shadows,*
Tourbillonnent dans l'extase	*Whirl wildly in the rapture*
D'une lune rose et grise,	*Of a pink and gray moon,*
Et la mandoline jase	*And the mandolin chatters on*
Parmi les frissons de brise.	*Amid the shivering breeze.*

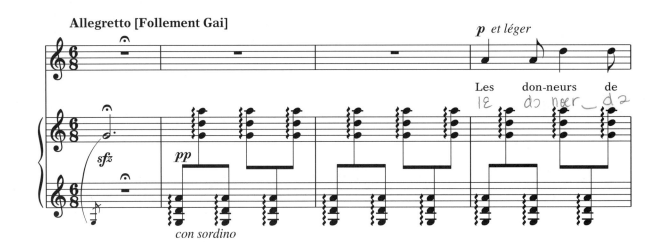

sé - ré - na - des   Et les bel - les é - cou-teu - ses   É - chan - gent

des pro-pos fa - des Sous les ra - mu-res chan - teu -

ses. _____   C'est Tir - cis et c'est _ A - min -

- te,   Et c'est l'é-ter-nel Cli - tan -

bleu - es, Tour - bil - lon - nent dans l'ex - ta - se

D'u - ne lu - ne rose et gri - se, Et la man - do -

li - ne ja - se par - mi les fris - sons de bri -

se. La, la, la, la, la

Noël des enfants qui n'ont plus de maisons

Claude Debussy

Claude Debussy
(1862-1918)

Composed 1915. Published by Durand & Cie, Paris, 1916; also Durand, 1916, in a version for piano and two sopranos. The manuscript for voice and piano as well as a version for children's chorus and piano are in the Bibliothèque Nationale, Paris. Jane Monjovet gave the first performance at a concert of the Amitiés franco-étrangères in the Grand Amphitheater of the Sorbonne, 9 April 1916. This is Debussy's last song, written to his own text on the eve of his first operation for the cancer that ended his life two years later. Enraged by the invasion of northern France by the German armies during World War I, he composed this personal protest. When Henri Büsser asked for permission to orchestrate the song, Debussy replied: "No, no, I have already refused it to André Caplet. I want this piece to be sung with the most discreet accompaniment. Not a word of this text must be lost, inspired as it is by the rapacity of our enemies. It is the only way I have to fight the war."

Noël des enfants qui n'ont plus de maisons	*Christmas carol for homeless children*
Nous n'avons plus de maisons!	*We have no homes!*
Les ennemis ont tout pris,	*The enemy has taken everything,*
tout pris, tout pris,	*everything, everything,*
jusqu'à notre petit lit!	*Even our little beds!*
Ils ont brûlé l'école et notre maître aussi.	*They have burned the school and our schoolmaster too.*
Ils ont brûlé l'église et monsieur Jésus-Christ	*They have burned the church and Mr. Jesus Christ*
Et le vieux pauvre qui n'a pas pu s'en aller!	*And the poor old man who could not get away!*
Nous n'avons plus de maisons!	*We have no homes!*
Les ennemis ont tout pris,	*The enemy has taken everything,*
tout pris, tout pris,	*everything, everything,*
jusqu'à notre petit lit!	*even our little beds!*
Bien sûr! Papa est à la guerre,	*Of course! Papa is away at war,*
Pauvre maman est morte!	*Poor Mama is dead!*
Avant d'avoir vu tout çà.	*Before she could see all of that.*
Qu'est-ce que l'on va faire?	*What are we to do now?*
Noël! Petit Noël! N'allez pas chez eux,	*Christmas! Little Father Christmas! Never visit their homes,*
n'allez plus jamais chez eux.	*never go to their homes again.*
Punissez-les!	*Punish them!*
Vengez les enfants de France!	*Avenge the children of France!*
Les petits Belges, les petits Serbes,	*The little Belgians, the little Serbs,*
et le petits Polonais aussi!	*and the little Poles too!*
Si nous en oublions, pardonnez-nous.	*If we've forgotten any, forgive us.*
Noël! Noël! surtout, pas de joujoux,	*Christmas! Father Christmas! above all no toys,*
Tâchez de nous redonner le pain quotidien.	*Try to give us again our daily bread.*
Noël! Ecoutez-nous,	*Christmas! Hear us,*
Nous n'avons plus de petits sabots:	*We have no little shoes left:*
Mais donnez la victoire aux enfants de France!	*But give victory to the children of France!*

Doux et triste (♩. = 144)

Nous n'a-vons plus de mai-sons!

Les en-ne-mis ont tout

pris, tout pris, tout pris, jus-qu'à no-tre pe-tit

lit! Ils ont brû-lé l'é-

sons!

Les en - ne - mis ont tout pris, tout pris, tout

decresc.

pris jus - qu'à no - tre pe - tit lit!

Ils ont brû - lé, l'é - cole et no - tre maître aus - si.

Nous n'a - vons plus de pe - tits sa - bots: _____

Tempo I

crescendo molto

Mais don - nez la vic - toire aux en - fants de

Fran - ce!

Après un rêve

Romain Bussine
(1830-1899)
After an anonymous Tuscan poet

Gabriel Fauré
(1845-1924)

Composed 1878? Op. 7, no. 1. The publisher, Hamelle added the opus number, at the request of Fauré, in 1896. Dedicated to Madame Marguerite Baugnies. Published by Choudens, 1878; Hamelle, 1887, first collection, no. 15. First performance, Société nationale de musique, 11 January 1879, Henriette Fuchs, soprano. Romain Bussine, professor of singing at the Paris Conservatoire, adapted the text from an Italian poem titled "Levati sol che la luna é levatai." It is written in an Italianate *bel canto* style, no doubt inspired by the Fauré's relationship with the Viardot family. Fauré was engaged to Marianne Viardot, daughter of Pauline Viardot (see "Fleur desséchée"). Marianne terminated the engagement, and Fauré composed this song—the evocation of a lost vision of love—soon after. Fauré's other Italianate settings ("Sérénade toscane," "Barcarolle" and "Chanson du pêcheur") also belong to this period. The popularity of this mélodie has occasioned many instrumental transcriptions.

Après un rêve

Dans un sommeil que charmait ton image
Je rêvais le bonheur, ardent mirage;
Tes yeux étaient plus doux, ta voix pure et sonore,
Tu rayonnais comme un ciel éclairé par l'aurore.

Tu m'appelais et je quittais la terre
Pour m'enfuir avec toi vers la lumière;
Les cieux pour nous, entr'ouvraient leurs nues,
Splendeurs inconnues, lueurs divines entrevues…

Hélas, hélas, triste réveil des songes!
Je t'appelle, ô nuit, rends-moi tes mensonges;
Reviens, reviens, radieuse,
Reviens, ô nuit mystérieuse!

After a dream

In a sleep charmed by your image
I dreamed of happiness,
Your eyes were soft, your voice pure and rich,
You were radiant as a sky lit by the dawn.

You called me, and I left the earth
To flee with you towards the light
The heavens parted their clouds for us
Unknown splendors, glimpses of divine light…

Alas, alas, sad awakening from dreams!
I call to you, o night, give me back your illusions;
Return, return in radiance,
Return, o mysterious night!

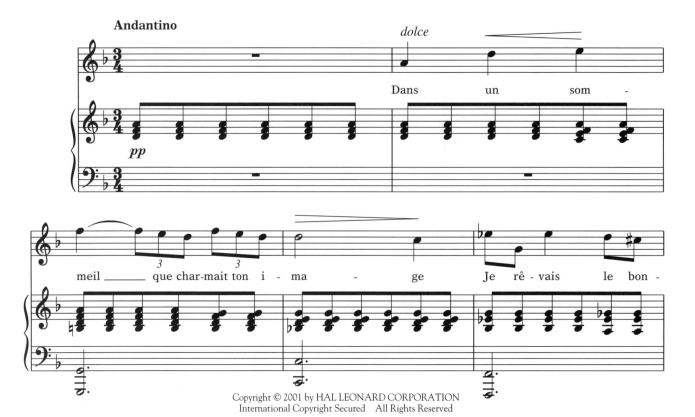

heur, ar-dent mi-ra - ge; Tes yeux é-taient plus

doux, _____ ta voix pure et so - no - - re, Tu ray - on -

nais comme un ciel _____ é-clai-ré par l'au - ro - re.

Tu m'ap-pe - lais _____ et je quit-tais la ter - re Pour m'en-fuir a - vec

toi vers la lu - miè - re; Les cieux _ pour _

nous, _ en - tr'ou - vraient leurs nu - es, Splen - deurs _ in - con -

nu - es, lu - eurs di - vi - nes en - tre - vu - es... Hé -

las, hé - las, tris - te ré - veil _ des son -

Chanson d'amour

Armand Silvestre
(1838-1901)

Gabriel Fauré
(1845-1924)

Composed 1882. Op. 27, no. 1. Dedicated to Madamoiselle Jane Huré. Published by Hamelle, 1882; second collection. no. 10. First performance: Société nationale de musique, 9 December 1882, Jane Huré, soprano. Armand Silvestre wrote graceful verse often criticized as sentimental and lacking in depth. However, composers such as Fauré and Duparc seemed able to work easily with his poetry. Fauré composed ten mélodies and one choral work using Silvestre's verses. In this setting, Fauré lengthened the poem by using the first four lines as a refrain.

Chanson d'amour	*Love Song*
J'aime tes yeux, j'aime ton front,	*I love your eyes, I love your forehead,*
O ma rebelle ô ma farouche,	*O my rebel, o my wild one,*
J'aime tes yeux, j'aime ta bouche	*I love your eyes, I love your mouth*
Où mes baisers s'épuiseront.	*Where my kisses will exhaust themselves.*
J'aime ta voix, j'aime l'étrange	*I love your voice, I love the strange*
Grâce de tout ce que tu dis,	*Grace of all you say,*
O ma rebelle, ô mon cher ange,	*O my rebel, o my darling angel*
Mon enfer et mon paradis!	*My hell and my paradise!*
J'aime tout ce qui te fait belle,	*I love everything that makes you beautiful,*
De tes pieds jusqu'à tes cheveux,	*From your feet to your hair,*
O toi vers qui montent mes vœux,	*O you towards whom all my desires fly,*
O ma farouche, ô ma rebelle!	*O my wild one, o my rebel!*

rouche, ô ma re-bel - le! J'ai - me tes yeux, j'ai - me ton front,

O ma re-belle, ô ma fa-rou - che, J'ai - me tes yeux, j'ai - me ta bou - che

Où mes bai-sers s'é-pui-se - ront. Où mes bai-sers s'é-pui-se - ront.

Clair de lune

Paul Verlaine
(1844-1896)

Gabriel Fauré
(1845-1924)

Composed 1887, Op. 46, no. 2. Dedicated to Monsieur Emmanuel Jadin. Published by Hamelle, 1888; second collection, no. 19; London, Metzler, 1897. Orchestrated by the composer in 1888. First performance, Société nationale de musique April 1888; Marice Bagès, tenor, with orchestra. The poem is taken from Verlaine's *Fêtes galantes* of 1869. Verlaine blends world of the *commedia dell'arte** with the atmosphere of the *Fêtes galantes* (romantic festivities) as depicted in eighteenth-century paintings by Watteau—scenes of charming, elegantly dressed couples, amusing themselves in great parks amidst fountains and statues (see "Mandoline"). Fauré always created an atmosphere or poetic mood in his songs, nowhere more elegantly than here—an extraordinary example of text and music that mutually enhance one another. This song was Fauré's first setting of Verlaine.

*The *commedia dell'arte* was a popular comedy form improvised by strolling players, using stock characters such as Columbine and Harlequin.

Clair de lune

Votre âme est un paysage choisi
Que vont charmant masques et bergamasques*
Jouant du luth et dansant et quasi
Tristes sous leurs déguisements fantasques.

Tout en chantant sur le mode mineur
L'amour vainqueur et la vie opportune,
Ils n'ont pas l'air de croire à leur bonheur
Et leur chanson se mêle au clair de lune.

Au calme clair de lune triste et beau,
Qui fait rêver les oiseaux dans les arbres
Et sangloter d'extase les jets d'eau,
Les grands jets d'eau sveltes parmi les marbres.

Moonlight

Your soul is a rare landscape
Charmed by masks and bergamasks
Playing the lute and dancing, and almost
Sad beneath their fantastic disguises.

While singing in the minor key
Of victorious love and the good life,
They do not seem to believe in their happiness,
And their song blends with the moonlight.

With the calm moonlight, sad and beautiful,
That makes the birds dream in the trees,
And the fountains sob with rapture,
The tall slender fountains among the marble statues.

*Although the term "bergamask" normally refers to a dance, Verlaine was apparently using the word to refer to those characters of the Italian comedy, such as Harlequin, who spoke in the dialect of Bergamo.

Jou - ant du luth et dan - sant et qua - si

Tris - tes sous leurs dé - gui - se - ments fan -

tas - ques.

dolce

Tout en chan - tant sur le mo-de mi - neur L'a-mour vain - queur ___

Lydia

Charles-Marie-René Leconte de Lisle
(1818-1894)

Gabriel Fauré
(1845-1924)

Composed c.1870. Op. 4, no. 2. Published by G. Hartmann, 1871; Choudens, 1877; Hamelle, 1887, first collection. no. 8. Dedicated to Mme. Marie Trélat. First performance, Société nationale de musique, 18 May 1872, Marie Trélat, mezzo-soprano. This is Fauré's first setting of Leconte de Lisle (see "Le Colibri"). De Lisle's poem in Hellenic style is elegant and beautifully balanced. Fauré mirrored its simplicity and antique mood by using the Lydian mode and simple vocal phrases with graceful curving lines. Fauré altered the poem slightly, probably to improve the vocal flow. "Chanter sur *tes lèvres* en fleur" was changed to "Chanter sur *ta lèvre* en fleur." In the first verse, Fauré omits the bracketed words in his setting: "Et sur ton col frais et si blanc / [Que le lait,] route étincelant." He gives the omitted words to the piano, which melodically initiates the phrase, removing the comparison of "white" and "milk." The song became personally significant when Fauré used its first measures as a recurring symbolic motif* in his song cycle *La bonne chanson* (1892-94).

*"Lydia" presumably referred to Emma Bardac, with whom Fauré was having an affair at the time he composed *La bonne chanson*.

Lydia

Lydia, sur tes roses joues,
Et sur ton col frais et si blanc,
[Que le lait,] roule étincelant
L'or fluide que tu dénoues.

Le jour qui luit est le meilleur;
Oublions l'éternelle tombe.
Laisse tes baisers, tes baisers de colombe
Chanter sur ta lèvre en fleur.

Un lys caché répand sans cesse
Une odeur divine en ton sein:
Les delices, comme un essaim
Sortent de toi, jeune Déesse!

Je t'aime meurs, ô mes amours,
Mon âme en baisers m'est ravie!
O Lydia, rends-moi la vie,
Que je puisse mourir toujours!

Lydia

Lydia, onto your rosy cheeks
And onto your neck, so fresh and white
There rolls down, gleaming
The flowing gold that you loosen.

The day that is dawning is the best;
Let us forget the eternal tomb.
Let your kisses, your dove-like kisses
Sing on your blossoming lips.

A hidden lily ceaselessly spreads
A divine scent in your bosom.
Delights, like swarming bees,
Emanate from you, young goddess!

I love you and die, oh my love,
My soul is ravished in kisses
O Lydia, give me back my life,
That I may die, die forever!

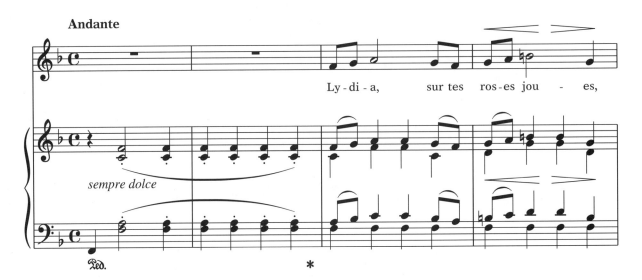

Et sur ton col frais et si* blanc, roule é-tin-ce-lant L'or flu-i-de ___ que tu dé-nou ___ es. Le jour qui luit est le meil-leur; Ou-bli-ons l'é-ter-nel-le tom - be. Lais-se tes bai-sers, tes bai-sers ___ de ___ co-lom - be

dolce

*"plus" in the original poem

*"tes lèvres" in the original poem

Je t'aime et meurs, ô mes a-mours, Mon âme en bai - sers _ m'est ra -

vi - e! O Ly - di - a, rends - moi _ la vi - e,

Que je puis - se mou-rir, mou - rir tou - jours!

Mandoline

Paul Verlaine
(1844-1896)

Gabriel Fauré
(1845-1924)

Composed 1891. Op. 58, no. 1 of *Cinq mélodies de Venise*. Dedicated to Madame la princesse Edmond de Polignac. Published by Hamelle, 1891; third collection, nos. 7-11. First performance, Société nationale de musique, 2 April 1892. Florent Schmitt orchestrated "Mandoline". Fauré began composing this set in Venice, while staying at the palazzo of the Princesse Edmond de Polignac, a great patron of contemporary music and art. The Princesse was formerly Winnaretta Singer, the sewing-machine heiress, who hosted one of the most elegant and influential salons in Paris. She was responsible for bringing Fauré and Verlaine together. "Mandoline," "En sourdine," and "A Clymène" are from Verlaine's collection of poems titled *Fêtes galantes*; "Green" and "C'est l'extase" come from his collection *Romances sans paroles*. Verlaine's flexible word rhythms created lyricism and fluidity in his verse, bringing back to French poetry musical qualities highly cultivated by the Renaissance poets (see Gounod's "O ma belle rebelle").

Mandoline

Les donneurs de sérénades
Et les belles écouteuses
Échangent des propos fades
Sous les ramures chanteuses.

C'est Tircis et c'est Aminte,
Et c'est l'éternel Clitandre,
Et c'est Damis qui pour mainte
Cruelle fait maint vers tendre.

Leurs courtes vestes de soie,
Leurs longues robes à queues,
Leur élégance, leur joie
Et leurs molles ombres bleues,

Tourbillonnent dans l'extase
D'une lune rose et grise,
Et la mandoline jase
Parmi les frissons de brise.

Mandolin

The serenaders
And their lovely listeners,
Exchange trivial banter
Under the singing boughs.

It is Tircis and Aminte,
And the tiresome Clitandre,
And Damis, who for many a
Cruel woman writes many a tender verse.

Their short silken jackets,
Their long dresses with trains
Their elegance, their merriment,
And their soft blue shadows,

Whirl wildly in the rapture
Of a pink and gray moon,
And the mandolin chatters on
Amid the shivering breeze.

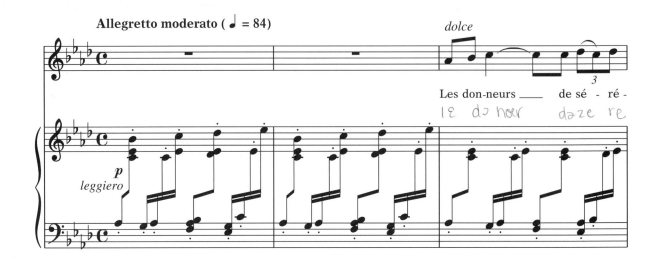

min - - te, Et c'est l'é - ter - nel Cli -

tan - dre, Et c'est Da - mis qui pour main - te Cru -

el - le fait* maint vers ten -

- dre. _____ Leurs cour - tes ves - tes de soie,

*"fit" in previous editions of the song; "fait" is true to the original poem

138

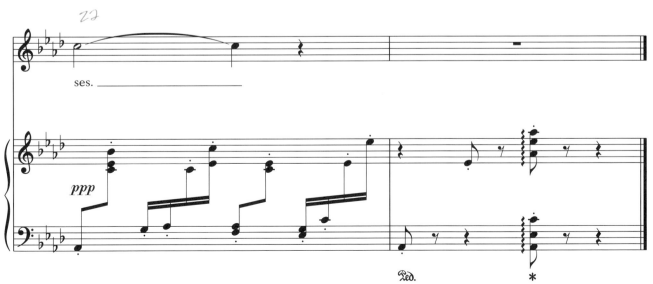

Notre amour

Armand Silvestre
(1838-1901)

Gabriel Fauré
(1845-1924)

Composed 1879? Op. 23, no. 2. Published by Hamelle, 1882, second collection, no. 81897. At the request of the composer, the opus number was added by the publisher, Hamelle, in 1896. Dedicated to Madame Castillon. The light texture and delicate colors found in this strophic song are reminiscent of Gounod. Many of Fauré's mélodies were first heard in salons in homes of patrons such as the Princesse de Polignac, where private musical performances were given for guests. The audience was comprised of writers, painters, musicians and representatives of high society. Most of the performers were talented amateurs. Fauré appreciated these singers and their sense of style and often dedicated his mélodies to them. He always argued that the voice should not have the "voluptuous" prestige of a solo instrument, but should be a *porte-verbe* (word carrier) with an exquisite timbre. The optional high note at the end of song originated with the composer, probably to flatter a particular singer.

Notre amour	Our love
Notre amour est chose légère	*Our love is a light thing,*
Comme les parfums que le vent	*Like the perfumes that the wind*
Prend aux cimes de la fougère,	*Brings from the tips of the ferns,*
Pour qu'on les respire en rêvant.	*And lets us breathe them and dream.*
Notre amour est chose charmante,	*Our love is a charming thing,*
Comme les chansons du matin,	*Like the songs of the morning*
Où nul regret ne se lamente,	*Where no sorrow is voiced,*
Où vibre un espoir incertain.	*Where an uncertain hope vibrates.*
Notre amour est chose sacrée,	*Our love is a sacred thing,*
Comme le mystères des bois	*Like the mysteries of the woods*
Où tressaille une âme ignorée,	*Where an unknown soul is throbbing,*
Où les silences ont des voix.	*Where silences have voices.*
Notre amour est chose infinie,	*Our love is an infinite thing,*
Comme le chemins des couchants,	*Like the paths of the sunsets,*
Où la mer, aux cieux réunie,	*Where the sea, reunited with the sky,*
S'endort sous les soleils penchants.	*Falls asleep beneath the setting suns.*
Notre amour est chose éternelle,	*Our love is an eternal thing,*
Comme tout ce qu'un dieu vainqueur	*Like everything that a conquering god*
A touché du feu de son aile.	*Touches with the fire of his wing.*
Comme tout ce qui vient du cœur.	*Like all that comes from the heart.*

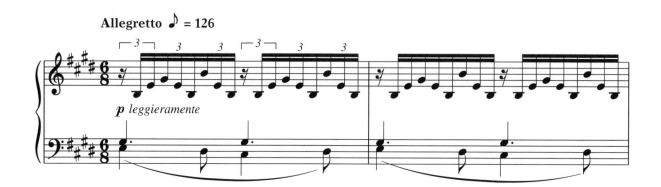

nul re-gret ne se la-men - te, Où vibre un es-poir in - cer-tain. Notre a -

mour est cho - se char-man - te!

Notre a-mour est cho - se sa-cré - e, Com-me les mys-tè - res des bois, Où tres-

saille une âme ig-no-ré - e, Où les si-len-ces ont des voix. Notre a -

mour est cho - se sa - cré - e!

dolce

Notre a-mour est chose in - fi - ni - e, Com - me les che-mins des cou-chants,

Où la mer, aux cieux ré - u - ni - e, S'en - dort sous les so-leils pen-chants.

nel - le, est __ chose __ é - ter -

ad lib.

nel - -

le! _____

*This optional note originated with the composer.

Automne

Armand Silvestre
(1838-1901)

Gabriel Fauré
(1845-1924)

Composed 1878, Opus 18, no. 3. Published by Hamelle, 1880; second collection, no. 3. First performance Société nationale de musique, 29 January 1881, Henrietta Fuchs, soprano. Dedicated to M. Emmanuel Jadin. In Fauré's catalogue, "Automne" stands out for its heavy dramatic texture and unrestrained climax. It is another example of Fauré's ability to compose an elegant, sustained melodic line underlaid with intense emotion (also see "Après un rêve").

Automne

Automne au ciel brumeux, aux horizons navrants
Aux rapides couchants, aux aurores pâlies,
Je regarde couler, comme l'eau du torrent,
Tes jours faits de mélancolie.

Sur l'aile des regrets mes esprits emportés,
Comme s'il se pouvait que notre âge renaisse!
Parcourent en rêvant les coteaux enchantés,
Où jadis, sourit ma jeunesse!

Je sens au clair soleil du souvenir vainqueur,
Refleurir en bouquet les roses déliées
En monter à mes yeux des larmes,
Qu'en mon cœur
Mes vingt ans avaient oubliées!

Autumn

Autumn of misty skies and heartbreaking horizons
Of fleeting sunsets, of pale dawns
I watch flowing by, like the waters of a torrent,
Your days tinged with melancholy.

My thoughts, carried away on the wings of regret,
—As though it were possible for our age to be reborn!
Travel in dreams over the enchanted hillsides,
Where once my youth had smiled!

In the bright sunlight of victorious memory
I smell the fallen roses blooming again in bouquets
And tears rise to my eyes
That in my heart
At twenty had been forgotten!

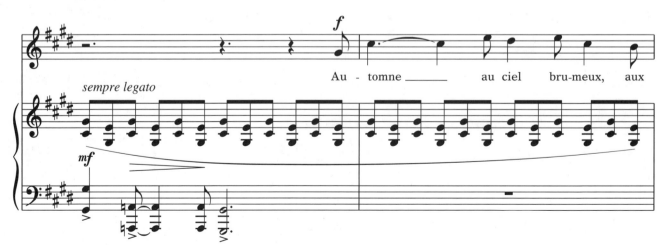

jours faits de mé-lan-co-li — e.

Sur l'ai - le des re-grets mes es -

prits em - por-tés, Com - me s'il se pou-vait que notre

â - ge re-nais - se! Par - cou - rent en rê-vant les co -

teaux __ en - chan-tés, Où ja - dis, ___ sou - rit ma jeu -

nes - se! _____ Je

sens, _____ au clair so - leil du sou - ve - nir vain-queur, _____

_____ Re - fleu - rir en bou-quets _____ les

L'absent

Charles Gounod

Charles Gounod
(1818-1893)

Composed 1876. Published by Choudens. In 1870 Gounod traveled to England and remained there until 1874. His wife returned to Paris long before he did. During this period, Gounod became embroiled in a drawn-out and scandalous liaison with Georgina Weldon, an infamous eccentric of the Victorian era. Among other endeavors, Mrs. Weldon ran a girls' orphanage. Lessons in singing were part of the education, and she resolved to have Gounod as composer-in-residence for her protégés. Gounod's affair with the disastrous Mrs. Weldon reached its tumultuous climax in the English courts. Georgina Weldon sued the composer, claiming monies she allegedly spent for supporting him while he composed. The case dragged on for years, but a jury ultimately awarded Mrs. Weldon £10,000 in damages. Gounod never paid, but could never return to England. During his sojourn in that country, he composed some sixty songs to English texts, including verses by Byron, Shelley, and Longfellow. Gounod composed the text and music for "L'absent" as a gesture of contrition to his wife after the Weldon affair.

L'absent

O silence des nuits dont la voix seule est douce,
Quand je n'ai plus sa voix,
Mystérieux rayons, qui glissez sur la mousse
Dans l'ombre de ses bois,

Dites-moi si ses yeux, à l'heure où tout sommeille
Se rouvrent doucement
Et si ma bien-aimée alors que moi je veille,
Se souvient de l'absent.

Quand la lune est aux cieux, baignant de sa lumière
Les grands bois est l'azure;
Quand des cloches du soir qui tintent la prière
Vibre l'écho si pur,

Dites-moi si son âme, un instant recueillie
S'élève avec leur chant,
Et si de leurs accords la paisible harmonie
Lui rappelle l'absent!

The Absent One

O silence of the night, whose voice alone is sweet
When I no longer hear her voice
Mysterious rays, gliding over the moss
In the shade of the woods—

Tell me if her eyes, at the hour when all sleeps
Reopen gently
And then if my beloved, when I am waking,
Remembers the absent one.

When the moon is in heaven, bathing with its light
The great forests and the sky;
When the evening bells, tolling for prayer
Awaken so pure an echo—

Tell me if her soul, musing for an instant
Raises her voice with their song,
And if the peaceful harmony of their sounds
Reminds her of the absent one!

douce, Quand je n'ai plus sa voix,_____

Mys - té - ri - eux ray - ons, qui glis - sez sur la

mous - se Dans l'om - bre de ses bois,_____

Di - tes-moi si ses yeux,_____ à l'heure où tout som -

Quand des clo - ches du soir qui tin - tent la pri - è - re

Vi - bre l'é - cho si pur, ___ l'é - cho si pur, ___

Di - tes-moi si son âme, un ins - tant re - cueil -

pp

p

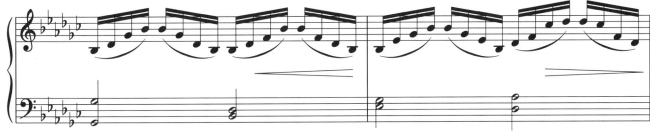

O ma belle rebelle

Jean-Antoine de Baïf
(1532-1589)

Charles Gounod
(1818-1893)

Composed 1855. Published by Choudens as no. 5 in *Vingt mélodies chant et piano par Charles Gounod* (1867). Jean-Antonoie de Baïf was a member of the Pléiade, a group of seven poets led by Pierre Ronsard who exalted and imitated the forms of classical antiquity as well as writing about the joys and tragedies of life in the 16th century. Baïf's poetry is especially notable for its innovative metrical schemes. He was especially interested in unrhymed lines and the possibilities for setting such verse to music. In 1570, with composer Thibaud de Courville, he founded *L'Académie de Poésie et de Musique*. The subject of this poem is Louise Labé, the most prolific French poetess of 16th century. She was born in Lyon around 1520 to a newly rich rope-maker's family and received an extensive liberal education. One of the many names by which she was called was "la Sappho lyonnaise." Her marriage to a wealthy rope-maker thirty years her senior caused many to refer to her as "La Belle Cordière." Her May-December marriage seems to have given her almost total freedom to socialize with men of letters and hold literary salons. Little is known about her admirers or her private life. One of her supposed lovers was the poet Clément Marot. Labé appears in Marot's collection of poems titled *L'Adolescence Clémentine* (1532), where she is referred to as "La belle rebelle."

O ma belle rebelle!	*O my beautiful rebel!*
Las! que tu m'es cruelle!	*Alas! how cruel you are to me*
Ou quand d'un doux souris,	*When with a sweet smile*
Larron de mes esprits,*	*That steals my spirit*
Ou quand d'une parole	*Or with a word*
Mignardètement* molle,	*Delicately soft,*
Ou quand d'un regard d'yeux	*Or with a glance from those eyes*
Fièrement* gracieux,	*Proudly graceful,*
Ou quand d'un petit geste,	*Or with the smallest gesture*
Tout divin, tout céleste*	*Quite divine, quite celestial*
En amoureuse ardeur	*You plunge all my heart*
Tu plonges tout mon cœur!	*Into ardent love!*
O ma belle rebelle!	*O my beautiful rebel!*
Las! que tu m'es cruelle!	*Alas! how cruel you are to me!*
Quand la cuisante ardeur	*When the fiery passion*
Qui me brûle* le cœur	*That consumes my heart*
Fait que je te demande	*Requires me to ask of you*
À sa brûlure* grande	*To cool the flames that burn me*
Un rafraîchissement*	*The refreshment*
D'un baiser seulement.	*Of a single kiss.*
O ma belle rebelle!	*O my beautiful rebel!*
Las! que tu m'es cruelle!	*Alas! how cruel you are to me!*
Quand d'un petit baiser	*When with one little kiss*
Tu ne veux m'apaiser.	*You will not appease me.*
Me puissé-je un jour, dure!	*Could I one day, heartless one!*
Venger* de ton injure,	*Avenge your insult*
Mon petit maître* Amour	*My young master, Cupid*
Te puisse outrer un jour,	*Would wound your heart some day*
Et pour moi* langoureuse	*And for me have you languish,*
Il te fasse* amoureuse,	*To cause you to love me*
Comme il m'a langoureux	*As he made me languish*
Pour toi* fait amoureux.	*And to love you.*
Alors par ma vengeance	*Thus through my vengeance*
Tu auras connaissance*	*You will know*
Quel mal fait, du baiser	*How harmful it is*
Un amant refuser.	*To refuse a lover a kiss.*

*These words have been changed to modern French spelling for this edition.

Andantino quasi Allegretto

O ma bel - le re - bel - le! Las!

que tu m'es cru - el - le! Ou quand d'un doux sou -

ris, Lar - ron de mes es - prits, Ou quand

162

-tit bai - ser Tu ne veux m'a - pai -

dim.

ser.

Me puis - sé - je un jour, du - re! Ven - ger de ton in -

pp

ju - re, Mon pe - tit maître A - mour Te puisse ou -

trer un jour, Et pour moi lan - gou -

reuse Il te fasse a - mou - reu - se, Comme

il m'a lan - gou - reux Pour toi fait a - mou -

reux. _____ A - lors par ma ven - gean -

Venise

Alfred de Musset
(1810-1857)

Charles Gounod
(1818-1893)

Composed 1842. Published by Choudens, 1867 (no. 9 in *Vingt mélodies chant et piano par Charles Gounod*). In 1855 Gounod arranged the song for four-hand accompaniment. Most of Gounod's songs were published in six volumes of twenty songs each, four collections by Choudens and two by Lemoine. Gounod, often referred to as the "father of the mélodie," composed over 200 songs, notable for their lyricism, elegant sense of proportion, and impeccable craftsmanship—characteristics that would influence Fauré. "Venise" is generally considered one of Gounod's finest mélodies. Alfred de Musset's lyrical verse pays homage to the Venice of Monteverdi. Gounod's musical reflection is a barcarole with a bravura piano introduction that also dances between strophes. It is an evocative illustration of "La Serenissima" at night, extolling the city's sensuous beauties and hidden delights. Musset's original poem had seventeen stanzas, of which Gounod set nos. 1, 5, 9, 10, and 15. The poet also provided Gounod with four extra stanzas (in the song, stanzas 5, 6, 8, and 9). In the version of the poem set by Gounod, the last strophe references the Austrian occupation of Venice after the Napoleonic wars. Musset rewrote the poem after 1866, updating the political situation.

Venise	*Venice*
Dans Venise la rouge,	*In Venice, the red*
Pas un bateau qui bouge,	*Not a boat is moving*
Pas un pêcheur dans l'eau,	*Not a fisherman on the water*
Pas un falot!	*Not a lantern!*
La lune qui s'efface	*The waning moon*
Couvre son front qui passe	*Covers her moving face*
D'un nuage étoilé	*With a starry cloud*
Demi-voilé!	*Half-veiled!*
Tout se tait, fors les gardes	*All is silent, save for the guards*
Aux longues hallebardes,	*With their long halberds*
Qui veillent aux créneaux	*Who keep watch over the battlements*
Des arsenaux.	*Of the arsenals.*
—Ah! maintenant plus d'une	*—Ah! now more than one maid*
Attend, au clair de lune,	*Waits, in the moonlight,*
Quelque jeune muguet,	*For somg young gallant,*
L'oreille au guet.	*Straining her ears.*
Sous la brise amoureuse	*Beneath the amorous breeze*
La Vanina rêveuse	*Dreamy Vanina*
Dans son berceau flottant	*In her floating cradle*
Passe en chantant;	*Glides by, singing;*
Tandis que pour la fête	*Meanwhile for the carnival*
Narcisse qui s'apprête,	*Narcissa prepares herself,*
Met, devant son miroir,	*Putting on, in front of her mirror,*
Le masque noir.	*The black mask.*
Laissons la vieille horloge,	*Let us leave the old clock,*
Au palais du vieux doge,	*At the venerable Doge's palace,*
Lui compter de ses nuits	*To count for him the boredom*
Les longs ennuis.	*Of his long nights.*
Sur sa mer nonchalante,	*On her carefree sea,*
Venise l'indolente	*Indolent Venice*
Ne compte ni ses jours	*Counts neither her days*
Ni ses amours.	*Nor her loves.*
Car Venise est si belle	*For Venice is so beautiful*
Qu'une chaîne, sur elle	*That a chain thrown round her*
Semble un collier jeté	*Resembles a necklace*
Sur la beauté.	*Adorning her beauty.*

168

169

lé, D'un nu - age é - toi - lé De - mi_____ voi -
veu - se Dans son ber -ceau flot -tant Passe ____ en_____ chan -
len - te Ne com -pte ni ses jours Ni_____ ses _____ a -

lé!_____
tant;_____ Tan -
mours._____

Tout _____ se tait, fors les gar - des Aux
dis_____ que pour _____ la fê - te Nar -
Car_____ Ve - nise est si bel - le Qu'u - ne

Nocturne

Louis de Fourcaud
(1851-1914)

César Franck
(1822-1890)

Composed 1884, Opus 85. 1884 (1885). Published by Enoch, 1900. Later orchestrated by J. Guy-Ropartz, a Franck disciple. César Franck's charismatic personality and talent for teaching established a legendary legacy. The devotion of his pupils—among them, Henri Duparc, Vincent d'Indy and Ernest Chausson—led to a founding of a school of composers. He composed only sixteen songs, but "Nocturne" is one of the finest. The poetic theme must have appealed to his sense of nobility and his interest in mysticism. Its broad-lined melody is somewhat reminiscent of the solemnity of some of Franck's organ works.

Nocturne

Ô fraîche nuit, nuit transparente,
Mystère sans obscurité,
La vie est noire et dévorante;
Ô fraîche nuit, nuit transparente,
Donne-moi ta placidité.

Ô belle nuit, nuit étoilée,
Vers moi tes regards sont baissés,
Éclaire mon âme troublée;
Ô belle nuit, nuit étoilée,
Mets ton sourire en mes pensers.

Ô sainte nuit, nuit taciturne,
Pleine de paix et de douceur,
Mon cœur bouillonne comme une urne;
Ô sainte nuit, nuit taciturne,
Fais le silence dans mon cœur.

Ô grande nuit, nuit solennelle,
En qui tout est délicieux.
Prends mon être entier sous ton aile;
Ô grande nuit, nuit solennelle,
Verse le sommeil en mes yeux.

Nocturne

O cool night, transparent night,
Mystery without obscurity,
Life is black and devouring;
O cool night, transparent night
Grant me your tranquility.

O lovely night, starry night
As you look down on me,
Bring light to my troubled soul,
O lovely night, starry night,
Let your smile enter my thoughts.

O holy night, silent night,
Full of peace and gentleness,
My heart seethes like a cauldron;
O holy night, silent night,
Bring silence to my heart.

O boundless night, solemn night,
In which all things give delight,
Take my whole being under your wing;
O boundless night, solemn night,
Pour sleep into my eyes.

-ne comme une ur -ne; Ô sain -te nuit,

dim.

nuit ta -ci-tur -ne, Fais _____ le si-len -ce dans mon

cœur.

un peu plus lent
molto dolce

Ô gran -de nuit, _____

nuit so -len-nel -le, En qui tout est dé -li -ci-

Offrande

Paul Verlaine
(1844-1896)

Reynaldo Hahn
(1875-1947)

Composed 1891. No. 8 in the first volume of 20 mélodies (*Premier volume de vingt mélodies*). Published 1895, Heugel. The composer's enigmatic dedication is "to ***." Hahn's mélodie is quite different from the settings of this poem by Fauré (*Cinq mélodies de Venise*) and Debussy (*Ariettes oubliées*). Both Debussy and Fauré's mélodies are more complex — breathless, ardent settings, richly textured. Hahn's "Offrande" is a subdued plea—quiet and intimate—with a simple transparent accompaniment. Verlaine's poem is called "Green;" the composer chose "Offrande" as the title of his setting. Although Hahn was only sixteen when he composed it, "Offrande" is considered to be one of his finest mélodies.

Offrande	*Offering*
Voici des fruits, des fleurs, des feuilles et des branches	*Here are fruits, flowers, leaves and branches*
Et puis voici mon coeur qui ne bat que pour vous.	*And here too is my heart that beats only for you.*
Ne le déchirez pas avec vos deux mains blanches	*Do not tear it with your two white hands*
Et qu'à vos yeux si beaux l'humble présent soit doux.	*And may this humble gift be sweet to your lovely eyes.*
J'arrive tout couvert encore de rosée	*I arrive covered with the dew*
Que le vent du matin vient glacer à mon front.	*That the morning wind iced on my brow*
Souffrez que ma fatigue à vos pieds reposée	*Let my fatigue, resting here at your feet*
Rêve des chers instants qui la délasseront.	*Dream of the lovely moments that will refresh it.*
Sur votre jeune sein laissez rouler ma tête	*On your young breast let me rest my head*
Toute sonore encor de vos derniers baisers;	*Still ringing with your last kisses,*
Laissez-la s'apaiser de la bonne tempête	*Let it be stilled after the sweet tempest*
Et que je dorme un peu puisque vous reposez.	*And let me sleep a little, while you rest.*

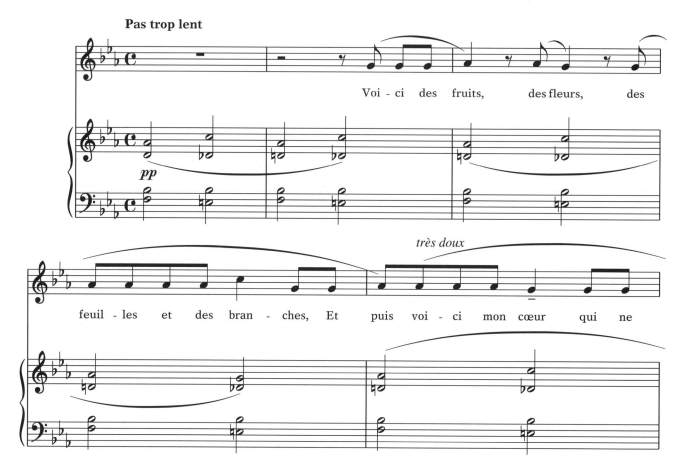

vent du ma - tin vient gla - cer à mon front. Souf -

frez que ma fa - tigue, à vos pieds re - po - sé - e

Rê - ve des chers in - stants ___ qui la dé - las - se - ront ___

très éteint

Sur vo - tre jeu - ne sein lais -

Si mes vers avaient des ailes

Victor Hugo
(1802-1885)

Reynaldo Hahn
(1875-1947)

Composed 1888, at age 13. . No. 2 in the first volume of 20 mélodies (*Premier volume de vingt mélodies*). Published 1895, Heugel. Dedicated to the composer's sister, Maria Hahn. Reynaldo Hahn was Venezuelan by birth, but came to Paris with his family at age four and made a brilliant career in France. He composed this mélodie, perhaps the most familiar of his songs, at age thirteen. Its fresh charm was clearly influenced by his teacher Jules Massenet. Hahn was a major figure in the cultural life of Paris during the *belle époque*. His mélodies capture the atmosphere of the Parisian salons where Hahn held forth, playing and singing his songs, frequently with a cigarette dangling from his lips. The art of singing was one of his major passions and preoccupations. Recent releases of historic Hahn recordings confirm his voice was small and somewhat bland, but his artistry in shaping musical material is rewarding to hear. He wrote three books on singing (*Du chant, Thèmes variés, L'oreille au guet*), as well as a memoir of Sarah Bernhardt. After 1912, Hahn composed in larger forms: opera, operetta, film music. His operetta *Ciboulette* (1923), perhaps his most famous work, is still performed and recorded.

Si mes vers avaient des ailes	*If my verses had wings*
Mes vers fuiraient, doux et frêles,	*My verses would fly, fragile and gentle,*
Vers votre jardin si beau,	*To your beautiful garden,*
Si mes vers avaient des ailes	*If my verses had wings*
Comme l'oiseau.	*Like a bird!*
Ils voleraient, étincelles,	*They would fly like sparks*
Vers votre foyer qui rit,	*To your cheery hearth,*
Si mes vers avaient des ailes	*If my verses had wings*
Comme l'esprit.	*Like my spirit.*
Près de vous, purs et fidèles,	*Pure and faithful, to your side*
Ils accourraient nuit et jour,	*They would hasten night and day*
Si mes vers avaient des ailes	*If my verses had wings*
Comme l'amour.	*Like love.*

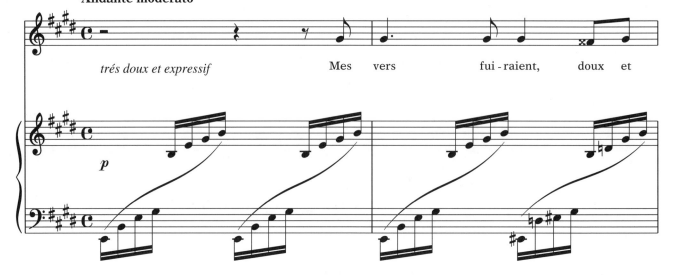

frê - les, _____ Vers vo - tre jar - din si

beau, _____ Si mes vers a -

vaient des ai - les Com - me l'oi -

seau. _____ Ils vo - le - raient, é - tin -

cel - les, _____ Vers vo - tre foy - er qui

rit, _____ Si mes vers a -

vaient des ai - les Com - me l'es -

prit. _____

Plus lent et en ralentissant jusqu'à la fin

Près de vous, purs et fi - dè - les, _____

Ils ac - cou - raient nuit et jour, _____

très retenu ... *encore plus lent* ... *long*

Si mes vers a - vaient des ai - les, Si mes vers a-vaient des

ai - les Com - me l'a - mour. _____

À Chloris

Théophile de Viau
(1590-1626)

Reynaldo Hahn
(1875-1947)

Composed 1916. Publisher: Heugel et Cie, 1921, No. 14 in *Deuxième volume de vingt mélodies*, the last major publication of Hahn's songs during his lifetime. In many of his later mélodies Hahn turned to a deliberately "archaic" style; "À Chloris" features Baroque musical characteristics. Like Fauré's setting of "Clair de lune," the accompaniment is a piano piece with its own ornamented melody and chaconne-like bass. The vocal line is subtly woven into the musical tapestry, creating a mood that is both declarative and intimate. Théophile de Viau was one of the most influential *libertin* poets of Louis XIII's reign. The *libertins'* verses had a particular charm that is immediately appealing but somewhat *précieux*. Despite its artificiality, de Viau's love poetry is not insipid, but full of evocative passion combined with elegant wit. De Viau died at the age of 36, after being denounced and imprisoned on morals charges for his bisexuality, and for writing licentious poetry. One of de Viau's well-known works for the theatre is *Pyrame et Thisbé* with a "plot within a plot" similar to the theme of Shakespeare's *A Midsummer Night's Dream*.

À Chloris	To Chloris
S'il est vrai, Chloris, que tu m'aimes,	*If it is true, Chloris, that you love me,*
Mais j'entends que tu m'aimes bien,	*And I have heard that you love me well,*
Je ne crois pas que les rois mêmes	*I do not believe that kings themselves*
Aient un bonheur pareil au mien.	*Can match such happiness as mine.*
Que la mort serait importune	*Even death would be powerless*
À venir changer ma fortune	*To come and change my fortune*
Pour la félicité des cieux!	*For all the joys of heaven!*
Tout ce qu'on dit de l'ambroisie	*All that is said of ambrosia*
Ne touche point ma fantaisie	*Does not touch my imagination*
Au prix des grâces de tes yeux.	*Like the grace of your eyes!*

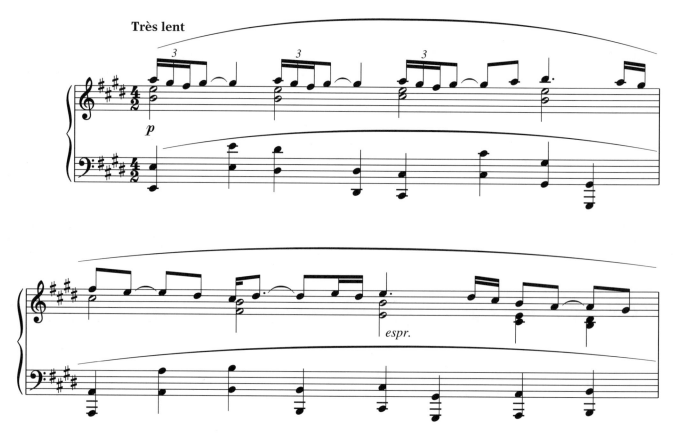

mê - mes _____ Aient un bon - heur _____ pa - reil _____ au

mien. _____

Que la

mort se - rait im - por - tu - ne À ve -

nir chan - ger ma for - tu - ne Pour la fé -

li - ci - té des cieux!

Tout ce qu'on dit de l'am - broi -

si - e Ne tou - che point ma fan - tai -

p

dim.

Madrigal

Robert de Bonnières
(1850-1905)

Vincent d'Indy
(1851-1931)

Composed 1872, Opus 4. Vincent d'Indy was born into a wealthy family of the nobility. A pupil of César Franck, d'Indy composed piano, chamber and orchestral works, operas, and songs. In 1894, he helped found the Schola Cantorum to perpetuate the musical tenets of Franck. He became its director in 1900. In 1912 he accepted the post of professor of orchestration at the Paris Conservatoire while still head of the Schola. He also taught conducting at the Conservatoire from 1914 to 1920. As a teacher he influenced two generations of French composers. Robert de Bonnières, French poet and man of letters, was a lifelong friend and collaborator of d'Indy, for whom he provided song texts and opera libretti. Bonniéres also collaborated with composer Henri Duparc, who set his poem "Le Manoir de Rosemonde." Never really comfortable with miniature forms, d'Indy wrote very few mélodies. "Madrigal," his second song for voice and piano, is a delicate setting in variation form. De Bonnière's rather static poem lends itself to d'Indy's simple but charming evocation of Renaissance music.

Madrigal	*Madrigal*
Qui jamais fut de plus charmant visage,	*Who ever had a more charming face*
De col plus blanc, de cheveux plus soyeux;	*A whiter neck, more silken hair,*
Qui jamais fut de plus gentil corsage,	*Who ever had a lovelier figure*
Qui jamais fut que ma Dame aux doux yeux!	*Who but my lady of the lovely eyes!*
Qui jamais eut lèvres plus souriantes,	*Who ever had more laughing lips*
Qui souriant rendit cœur plus joyeux,	*Whose smile made the heart more joyous*
Plus chaste sein sous guimpes transparentes,	*Had a more chaste bosom beneath filmy bodice*
Qui jamais eut que ma Dame aux doux yeux!	*Who but my lady of the lovely eyes!*
Qui jamais eut voix d'un plus doux entendre,	*Who ever had a voice sweeter to hear*
Mignonnes dents qui bouche emperlent mieux;	*Or whiter teeth shining like pearls;*
Qui jamais fut de regarder si tendre,	*Who ever had a look more tender,*
Qui jamais fut que ma Dame aux doux yeux!	*Who but my lady of the lovely eyes!*

194

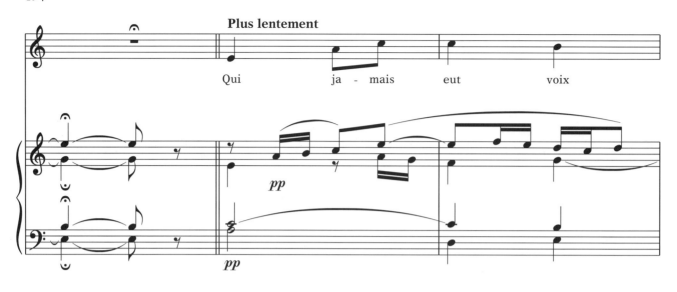

Plus lentement

Qui ja - mais eut voix

d'un plus doux en - ten - dre, Mi - gnon - nes

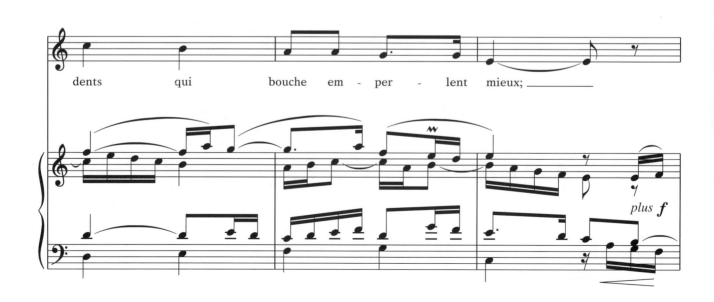

dents qui bouche em - per - lent mieux;

Si tu le veux

Maurice de Marsan

Charles Koechlin
(1867-1950)

Composed 1894, Op. 5, no. 5. Charles Koechlin, a student of Gabriel Fauré (see Fauré) at the Conservatoire, was an enigmatic musical figure. His compositional style was eclectic and often eccentric. In some respects, Koechlin shared similarities with Charles Ives in his musical experimentation and his admiration for the transcendental philosophies of Emerson and Thoreau. Koechlin's songs have vocal lines that approximate speech patterns, lacking the glamour of arching melodic phrases. He was inventive in choosing texts; however, many verses he chose to set as songs were long and complex. Late in life, his adoration for Lillian Harvey, a film actress of the 1930s, produced 113 piano pieces and a song cycle. One song, "Keep that school girl complexion," is based on a Palmolive soap ad Koechlin saw during a trip to the United States. Koechlin is better remembered and respected as a writer, theorist, orchestrator and teacher; students included Francis Poulenc, Germaine Tailleferre, and the École d'Arcueil, a group of four composers organized by Satie as successors to Les Six.

Si tu le veux

Si tu le veux, ô mon amour,
Ce soir dès que la fin du jour
Sera venue,
Quand les étoiles surgiront,
Et mettront des clous d'or au fond
Bleu de la nue,
Nous partirons seuls tous les deux
Dans la nuit brune en amoureux,
Sans qu'on nous voie,
Et tendrement je te dirai
Un chant d'amour où je mettrai
Toute ma joie.

Mais quand tu rentreras chez toi,
Si l'on te demande pourquoi,
Mignonne fée,
Tes cheveux sont plus fous qu'avant,
Tu répondras que seul le vent
T'a décoiffée,
Si tu le veux, ô mon amour.

If you wish

If you wish, o my love
This evening, as soon as day
Has ended,
When the stars come out
And shine like golden nails
In the door of the blue sky
We two shall go alone,
As lovers into the dark night
Unseen by anyone,
And tenderly I shall sing
A song of love into which I'll pour
All my joy.

But when you return home,
If anyone asks you why,
Sweet enchantress,
Your hair is more tousled than it was,
You need only answer that the wind
Has blown it about
If you want, o my love.

Allegro con moto

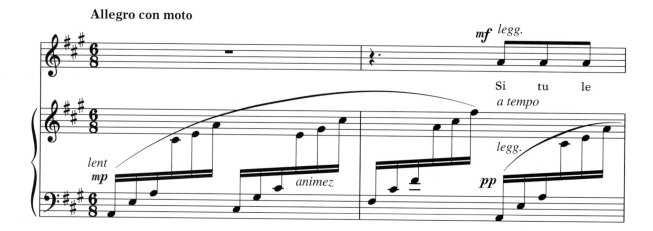

Nuit d'Espagne

Louis Gallet
(1835-1898)

Jules Massenet
(1842-1912)

Composed 1872. Massenet based this song on the *Air de ballet* from his orchestral suite *Scènes pittoresques*. Its energetic rhythmic accompaniment, describing a sultry evening, is derived from Spanish dance figures woven into a colorful texture that almost upstages the voice. Louis Gallet originally titled his poem "L'heure d'amour." Massenet's "Elégie" is another setting of a Gallet poem.

Nuit d'Espagne	Spanish Night
L'air est embaumé,	The air is balmy,
La nuit est sereine	The night is serene
Et mon âme est pleine	And my soul is full
De pensers joyeux;	Of joyous thoughts;
Viens! ô bien aimée!	Come! my beloved!
Voici l'instant de l'amour!	This is the moment of love!
Dans les bois profonds,	Into the deep woods,
Où les fleurs s'endorment,	Where the flowers sleep,
Où chantent les sources;	Where the springs are singing;
Vite enfuyons nous!	Let us go quickly!
Vois, la lune est claire	Look, the moon is bright,
Et nous sourit dans le ciel,	And smiling in the sky,
Les yeux indiscrets	Prying eyes
Ne sont plus à craindre,	Are no longer to be feared
Viens! ô bien aimée!	Come! my beloved!
La nuit protège ton front rougissant!	The night covers your blushing face!
La nuit est sereine,	The night is serene
Apaise mon cœur!	Calm my heart!
Viens! ô bien aimée!	Come! my beloved!
C'est l'heure d'amour!	It is the hour of love!
Dans le sombre azur,	In the dark blue sky
Les blondes étoiles	The pale stars
Écartent leur voiles	Cast off their veils
Pour te voir passer,	To see you pass by,
Viens! ô bien aimée!	Come! my beloved!
Voici l'instant de l'amour!	This is the moment of love!
J'ai vu s'entr'ouvrir	I saw, half open
Ton rideau de gaze.	Your gauzy curtain
Tu m'entends, cruelle,	You hear me, cruel one,
Et tu ne viens pas!	And you do not come!
Vois, la route est sombre	Look, the path is dark
Sous les rameaux enlacés!	Under the intertwined branches!
Cueille en leur splendeur	Gather in their splendor
Tes jeunes années,	Your youthful years,
Viens! car l'heure est brève,	Come! Time is short,
Un jour effeuille les fleurs du printemps!	In one day the leaves of spring are shed
La nuit est sereine, apaise mon cœur!	The night is serene, calm my heart!
Viens! ô bien aimée!	Come! o my beloved!

202

Allegretto quasi Andantino

très marqué

dim.   *p*   *pp* poco rall.

avec charme et nonchalance

a tempo

L'air est em-bau-

mé,   La nuit est se-rei - ne   Et mon âme est

plei - ne De pen-sers joy-eux;   ô bien ai-mé - e,

re!

a tempo

f très marqué

dim.   *p*   *pp poco rit.*   *a tempo* *pp*

pp

Dans le sombre a - zur,   Les blon-des é - toi - les

É - car-tent leurs voi - les Pour te voir pas - ser,   ô bien ai - mé - e,

Viens! ô bien ai - mé - e! Voi - ci l'ins - tant __ de l'a - mour! __

J'ai vu s'en - tr'ou -

vrir Ton ri - deau de ga - ze. Tu m'en - tends, cru -

elle, Et tu ne viens pas, tu ne viens pas! Vois, la route est

Si tu veux, Mignonne

Abbé Claude Georges Boyer
(1618-1698)

Jules Massenet
(1842-1912)

Composed 1876. Although Massenet is more remembered for his prodigious output of operas rather than for his mélodies, he composed over 250 songs. His songs cover a wide range of subjects and emotions; they are dramatically conceived and often have an operatic vocal quality. Many are dedicated to famous singers of the time. Massenet has been called Gounod's true successor in the development of the mélodie. Like Gounod, Massenet perfected the salon style in his song, and passed this on to his pupil, Reynaldo Hahn (see Hahn).

Si tu veux, Mignonne

If you wish, Mignonne

Si tu veux, Mignonne, au printemps
Nous verrons fleurir l'aubépine,
Qui sème dans les prés naissants
La neige de sa tête fine,
Si tu veux, Mignonne, au printemps
Nous verrons fleurir l'aubépine!

If you wish, Mignonne, in the spring
We will see the hawthorn flower,
Scattering in the fresh meadows
The snow from its delicate head,
If you like, Mignonne, in the spring
We will see the hawthorn flower!

Si tu veux, quand viendra l'été,
Nous écouterons dans les branches
Les chants d'amour et de gaîté
Des petites colombes blanches,
Si tu veux, quand viendra l'été,
Nous écouterons dans les branches!

If you like, when the summer comes
We will listen amidst the branches
To the joyous love songs
Of the little white doves,
If you like, when the summer comes,
We will listen amidst the branches!

Nous irons dans le bois jaunis,
Si tu veux, quand viendra l'automne,
Pour qu'elles aient chaud dans leurs nids
Leur porter des brins d'anémone,
Si tu veux, Mignonne,
Nous irons dans les bois jaunis
Quand viendra l'automne…

We will walk in the yellowed woods,
If you want, when autumn comes
So the birds will be warm in their nests
We will take them sprigs of anemones
If you wish, Mignonne,
We will walk in the yellowed woods,
When autumn comes…

Et puis, quand reviendra l'hiver…
Nous nous ressouviendrons des roses,
Du printemps, et du sentier vert
Où tu m'as juré tant de choses!
Alors…quand reviendra l'hiver…
Nous nous ressouviendrons des roses!
Si tu veux, Mignonne!

And then, when winter comes again
We will recall again the roses
Of spring, and the green path
Where you promised so many things to me!
When winter comes again…
We will recall again the roses!
If you wish, Mignonne!

Très animé et soutenu

Si tu veux, Mi - gnonne, au prin - temps Nous ver-rons fleu - rir l'au-bé - pi - ne, Qui sè - me dans les prés nais - sants La nei - ge de sa tê - te fi - ne, Si tu veux, Mi-gnonne, au prin - temps Nous ver-rons fleu - rir l'au-bé - pi -

toujours soutenu et doux

poco rall.
dim
a tempo
suivez
a tempo

Oh! quand je dors

Victor Hugo
(1802-1885)

Franz Liszt
(1811-1886)

Composed 1842 (version 1), 1859 (version 2). Version 1 published 1844; version. 2, 1860. In 1847, the composer created a piano transcription of this song, which is unpublished. Liszt set this poem twice; the first version (1842) featured an overly virtuoso piano accompaniment. For the second version, Liszt reduced the complex accompaniment texture to a simpler arpeggiation, highlighting the fluidity of the piano and vocal phrases and emphasizing the intimacy of Hugo's verse. The 1859 version, published here, is the far more often performed version. Liszt composed more than 80 songs, plus more than 20 extra versions and new settings. "Oh! quand je dors" is one of his best-known songs, and is considered the masterpiece among his fourteen French mélodies. He captures the passionate imagery of Hugo's verse in a rhapsodic setting that seems to be spontaneously improvised. In general, Liszt's musical settings of French texts show more affinity with the German Lied than the French mélodie.

Oh! quand je dors

Oh! quand je dors, viens auprès de ma couche,
Comme à Pétrarque apparaissait Laura,
Et qu'en passant ton haleine me touche…—
    Soudain ma bouche
    S'entr'ouvrira!

Sur mon front morne où peut-être s'achève
Un songe noir qui trop longtemps dura,
Que ton regard comme un astre s'élève…—
    Soudain mon rêve
    Rayonnera!

Puis sur ma lèvre où voltige une flamme,
Éclair d'amour que Dieu même épura,
Pose un baiser, et d'ange deviens femme…—
    Soudaine mon âme
    S'éveillera!

Oh viens! comme à Pétrarque apparaissait Laura!

Oh! while I sleep

Oh! while I sleep, come to my bedside
Just as Laura appeared to Petrarch
And in passing, let your breath touch me…
    Suddenly my lips
    Will part!

On my troubled brow, where a dark dream
That lasted too long is perhaps ending
Let your gaze fall like a star. . .
    Suddenly my dream
    Will become radiant!

Then on my lips, where a flame flickers
A flash of love which God made pure,
Place a kiss, and from angel become woman…
    Suddenly my soul
    Will awaken!

Oh come! just as Laura appeared to Petrarch!

viens au-près de ma cou - che, Comme à Pé - trarque

smorz.

ap - pa - rais - sait Lau - ra,

sempre dolciss.

Et qu'en pas - sant

sempre pp

ton ha-lei - ne me tou - che... Sou-dain ma bou - che

flam - me, É-clair d'a - mour _____ que

Dieu même _____ é - pu - ra,

poco rall.
pp
poco rit.

Pose _____ un bai - ser, et d'an - ge _ de - viens

ppp *poco rall.* *poco rit.*

a tempo *rinforzando*
cresc.

fem - me... Sou - daine mon â - me S'é - veil - le -

a tempo *f*

tre corde

Plaisir d'amour

Jean-Pierre Claris de Florian
(1755-1794)

Johann-Paul Martini
(1741-1816)

This *romance* was composed in 1784 in Nancy, and published the following year as a supplement to the novella *Célestine*. Martini was a German composer who moved to France in 1760 and spent most of his career there. He eventually became well-known for writing opera. He is cited as the first composer in France to compose songs with piano accompaniment rather than continuo. He is most remembered for "Plaisir d'amour," a classic *romance* that remains a famous prototype of the style. The *romance* evolved from earlier French poetic-vocal forms, notably those of the troubadours. Eighteenth-century *romances* were strophic in form, with simple melodic lines that were sung without affectation. Accompaniments were subordinate to the vocal line and there was little or no musical interaction between voice and piano. "Plaisir d'amour" is notable for its rondo form and more involved accompaniment, which features a prelude, interlude, and postlude.

Plaisir d'amour	*The pleasures of love*
Plaisir d'amour ne dure qu'un moment,	*The pleasures of love last but a moment*
Chagrin d'amour dure toute la vie.	*The sorrows of love last all life through.*
J'ai tout quitté pour l'ingrate Sylvie,	*I have given up everything for the ungrateful Sylvia*
Elle me quitte et prend un autre amant.	*She left me and took another lover.*
Plaisir d'amour ne dure qu'un moment,	*The pleasures of love last but a moment*
Chagrin d'amour dure toute la vie.	*The sorrows of love last all life through.*
Tant que cette eau coulera doucement	*As long as this water runs gently*
Vers ce ruisseau qui borde la prairie,	*Towards the brook that borders the meadow,*
Je t'aimerai, me répétait Sylvie.	*I shall love you, Sylvia told me.*
L'eau coule encor, elle a changé pourtant.	*The stream still flows, but she has changed.*
Plaisir d'amour ne dure qu'un moment,	*The pleasures of love last but a moment,*
Chagrin d'amour dure toute la vie.	*The sorrows of love last all life through.*

Plai - sir d'a - mour ____ ne du - re qu'un ___ mo - ment, ____ Cha -

grin d'a - mour du - re tou - te la vi -

e. J'ai tout quit - té pour l'in - gra - te Syl -

mour du - re tou - te la vi - e.

Tant que cette eau cou - le -

ra dou - ce - ment Vers

ce ruis - seau qui bor - de la prai - ri - e,

Dans un bois solitaire

Antoine Houdar de la Motte

Wolfgang Amadeus Mozart
(1756-1791)

Ariette, K. 308, composed 1778 in Mannheim. This is one of two *ariettes* that Mozart composed to French text; the other is "Oiseaux, si tous les ans," K. 307. Both are deliberate imitations of the French *chanson*. Mozart called them "Freundstücke" (offerings to friends). Enroute to Paris in 1778, Mozart stopped for a prolonged visit in the home of Johann Baptist Wendling, the great Mannheim flautist. Mozart composed the two songs as "house gifts" for the Wendling's daughter Augusta ("Gustl"), who chose the texts. In a letter to his father, Mozart related that Miss Wendling performed them "incomparably well." Mozart attached little significance to the songs, intending them as material for an evening's entertainment; however, his unerring sense of drama created little masterpieces. "Dans un bois solitaire" is a through-composed miniature drama. The dramatic content of this poetry appealed to Mozart, who used a fluid mixture of aria and arioso in his setting. Distinguished Mozart biographer Alfred Einstein called this song "Watteau in music" and rightly so; its style is full of French elegance and charm.

Dans un bois solitaire	In a lonely wood
Dans un bois solitaire et sombre	In a dark and lonely wood
Je me promenais l'autr'jour,	I walked the other day,
Un enfant y dormait l'ombre;	A child was sleeping in the shadows;
C'était le redoutable Amour.	It was the formidable Cupid himself.
J'approche, sa beauté me flatte,	I approached, his beauty charmed me,
Mais je devais m'en défier;	But I should have resisted ;
Il avait les traits d'une ingrate,	He had all the features of a faithless one
Que j'avais juré d'oublier.	Whom I had sworn to forget.
Il avait la bouche vermeille,	He had the same crimson mouth
Le teint aussi frais que le sien,	The same fresh complexion as hers,
Un soupir m'échappe, il s'éveille;	A sigh escaped me, he awoke;
L'amour se réveille de rien.	Cupid wakes at anything.
Aussitôt deployant ses ailes et saisissant	Spreading his wings at once and seizing
Son arc vengeur,	His vengeful bow,
L'une de ses flêches, cruelles en partant,	He shoots one of his cruel arrows,
Il me blesse au cœur.	And he wounds me to the heart.
Va! va, dit-il, aux pieds de Sylvie,	"Go," he said, "to Sylvie's feet,
De nouveau languir et brûler!	To languish and burn again!
Tu l'aimeras toute ta vie,	You shall love her all your life
Pour avoir osé m'éveiller.	For having dared to wake me."

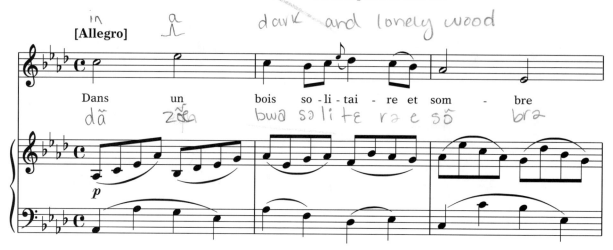

Psyché

Pierre Corneille
(1606-1684)

Emile Paladilhe
(1844-1926)

Composed 1884. Emile Paladilhe, winner of the Prix de Rome in 1860, composed two volumes of published mélodies, but is really remembered for just one, "Psyché." The romantic Greek myth of Cupid and Psyche is found in Apuleius' *Metamorphoses*. The lovelorn Psyche daunted all suitors with her great beauty. People ceased worshipping Venus and turned their adoration to Psyche. Enraged, Venus vowed vengeance and ordered her son Cupid to make Psyche fall in love with the ugliest creature he could find. When he saw Psyche, he fell in love with her himself. In his story Apuleius hints at an allegory of the soul (psyche) in pursuit of divine love (eros). This poem was also set by Koechlin (see "Si tu le veux").

Psyché

Je suis jaloux, Psyché, de toute la nature:
Les rayons du soleil vous baisent trop souvent;
Vos cheveux souffrent trop les caresses du vent:
   Quand il tes flatte, j'en murmure;
   L'air même que vous respirez
Avec trop de plaisir passe votre bouche;
   Votre habit de trop près vous touche;
   Et sitôt que vous soupirez,
   Je ne sais quoi qui m'effarouche
Craint parmi vos soupirs des soupires égares.

Psyche

I am jealous, Psyche, of all nature:
The sun's rays kiss you far too often;
Your hair too often accepts the wind's caresses:
   When he blows your hair, I am jealous;
   Even the air you breathe
Passes your lips with too much pleasure;
   Your garment touches you too closely;
   And whenever you sigh,
   I do not know what frightens me
Perhaps that your sighs are not all meant for me.

Andante quasi Andantino

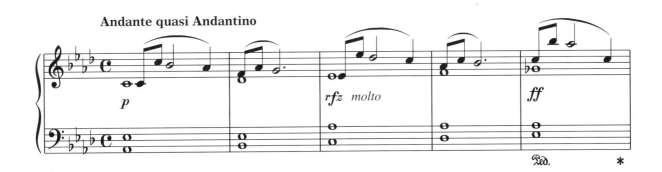

loux, Psy-ché, de tou-te la na-tu — re: Les ra-yons du so-

cresc.

f

leil — vous bai-sent trop sou-vent; Vos che-veux souf-frent trop des ca-res-ses du

dim. p p

vent: Quand il tes flat-te, j'en mur-mu — re; L'air mê — me que vous res-pi-

opt.

p

rez — A-vec trop de plai-sir pas-se sur vo-tre bou — che; Votre ha-

rfz

f dim. p

Le Bestiaire
ou Cortège d'Orphée

Guillaume Apollinaire
(1880-1918)

Francis Poulenc
(1899-1963)

The Book of Beasts
or Procession of Orpheus

Le dromadaire
La chèvre du Thibet
La sauterelle
Le dauphin
L'écrevisse
La carpe

Composed 1918-1919 for low voice and chamber orchestra (flute, clarinet, bassoon, string quartet). Publisher: Max Eschig, 1920. Poulenc created a version for piano and voice, and it is in this form the work is usually performed. The work is dedicated to composer Louis Durey, a member of Les Six (with Francis Poulenc, Darius Milhaud, Georges Auric, Germaine Tailleferre and Arthur Honegger), who also set the poems of *Le Bestiaire*. The first performance was sung by Poulenc's good friend, soprano Suzanne Peignot. "J'aime la voix humaine!" is a much-quoted statement of Francis Poulenc, whose love for the singing voice created the largest body of songs to be added to French vocal literature in the 20th century. *Le Bestiaire* is Poulenc's earliest cycle, composed when he was barely twenty years old, and is also one of his most familiar vocal works. He said: "From *Bestiaire* onwards, I felt a definite and mysterious affinity with Apollinaire's poetry." This marked his first setting of Apollinaire, who was to inspire thirty-five more songs and cycles and Poulenc's first opera *Les Mamelles des Tirésias* (1944).

 Guillaume Apollinaire's interest in writing a series of quatrains about a bestiary was sparked by a series of woodcuts by Pablo Picasso. Apollinaire eventually wrote thirty poems, describing his collection as "one of the most varied, seductive and accomplished poetical works of the new lyric generation." He planned an illustrated edition; Picasso was involved in other projects, so Apollinaire chose artist Raoul Dufy to create a series of woodcuts. Dufy's lively humorous woodcuts for *Le Bestiaire* were his first published illustrations. *Le Bestiaire* was finally published in Paris by Deplanche, February, 1911. Of the publisher's run of one hundred twenty copies, only about fifty were sold at 100 francs apiece. The remaining copies were sent to a second-hand book dealer who lowered the price to 40 francs. According to Dufy, Apollinaire and Dufy eventually realized only about 100 francs apiece from the work. The original Deplanche publication of *Le Bestiaire* is now considered one of the masterpieces of twentieth-century book production.

 In 1918, a reprint of the Apollinaire-Dufy publication inspired Poulenc to compose *Le Bestiaire*. Poulenc originally set twelve poems, but on the advice of his friend, composer Georges Auric, kept only six. Two of the rejected mélodies may be found in the Bibliothèque Nationale in Paris: "Le Serpent" (The Snake) and "La Colombe" (The Dove). Years later, Poulenc returned again to the collection to set "La Souris" (The Mouse) as a birthday gift for Marya Freund on her eightieth birthday. Poulenc referred to the tone of Apollinaire's work as "both melancholy and joyous." The cycle is lyric and lighthearted but also pensive and droll—a gentle reminder that humans share the foibles of animals, fish and fowl. The miniature proportions of the cycle give it an intimate quality and an astonishing unity. The piano accompaniments, based on ostinato patterns, provide dramatic background as well as commentary on the texts. From the plodding gait of the explorer's camels to the languid carp swimming in his pool, a varied and colorful parade passes by.

 Poulenc's flair for the dramatic is apparent even in these early miniatures, and despite their brevity, one can already hear the lyricism that became an integral part of his song style. Writing of this cycle in his *Journal de mes melodies*, the compser declared these first songs as already "typical Poulenc." He also added a note of caution for the performer: "To sing *Le Bestiaire* with irony and above all knowingly is a complete misconception, showing no understanding whatsoever of Apollinaire's poetry or my music."

 The songs of the cycle are in the original keys in the Low edition, and transposed for the High edition, with the exception of "La sauterelle."

Le dromadaire

Le dromadaire

Avec ses quatre dromadaires
Don Pedro d'Alfaroubeira
Courut le monde et l'admira.
Il fit ce que je voudrais faire
Si j'avais quatre dromadaires.

The Dromedary

With his four dromedaries
Don Pedro d' Alfaroubeira
Traveled the world over and admired it.
He did what I would like to do
If I had four dromedaries.

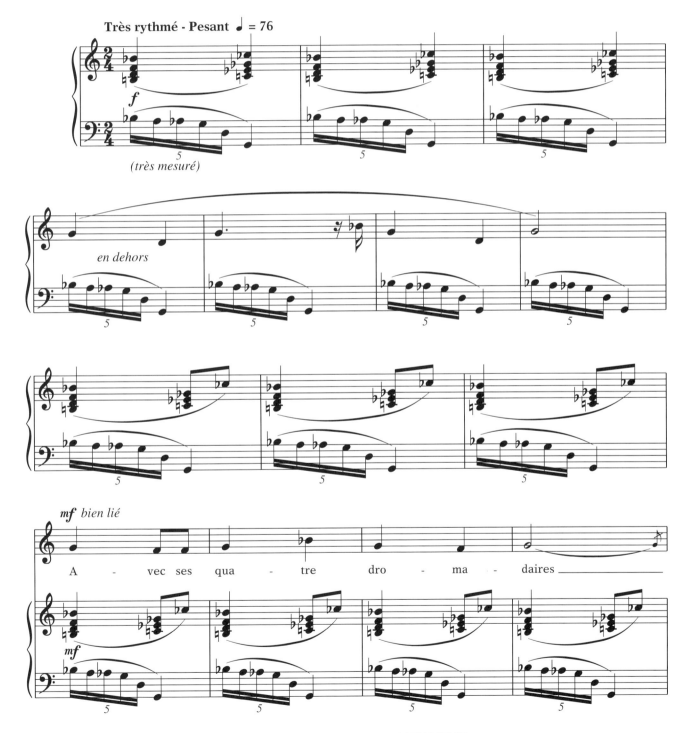

Don Pe - dro d'Al - fa - rou - bei - ra

Cou - rut le monde et l'ad - mi - ra.

Il fit ce

La chèvre du Thibet

La chèvre du Thibet

Les poils de cette chèvre et même
Ceux d'or pour qui prit tant de peine
Jason ne valent rien qu prix
Des cheveux dont je suis épris.

The Tibetan Goat

The hair of this goat and even
The golden hair for which such pains were taken
By Jason are worth nothing compared
To the hair of the one I love.

La sauterelle

La sauterelle

Voici la fine sauterelle,
La nourriture de Saint Jean,
Puissent mes vers être comme elle
Le régal des meilleures gens.

The Grasshopper

Here is the delicate grasshopper,
The nourishment of Saint John,
May my verses likewise be
A feast for superior people.

Le dauphin

Le dauphin

Dauphins, vous jouez dans la mer,
Mais le flot est toujours amer.
Parfois, ma joie éclate-t'elle?
La vie est encore cruelle.

The Dolphin

Dolphins, you play in the sea,
But the waves are always briny.
Does my joy burst forth at times?
Life is still cruel.

Animé ♩ = 136

mf

sans pédale

très souple

Dau - phins, vous jou - ez dans la mer, Mais le flot est tou -

jours a - mer. Par - fois ma joie é - cla - te t'elle?

La vie est en-co-re cru - el - le.

ralentir

mf

L'écrevisse

L'écrevisse

Incertitude, ô mes délices
Vous et moi nous nous en allons
Comme s'en vont les écrevisses,
À reculons, à reculons.

The Crayfish

Uncertainy, Oh! my delights,
You and I, we progress
As crayfish do,
Backwards, backwards.

La carpe

La carpe

Dans vos viviers, dans vos étangs,
Carpes, que vous vivez longtemps!
Est-ce que la mort vous oublie,
Poissons de la mélancolie

The Carp

In your pools, in your ponds,
Carp, you live such a long time!
Is it that death has passed you by,
Fish of melancholy?

Dans vos vi-viers, dans vos è-tangs, Car-pes, que vous vi-vez long-temps! Est-ce que la mort vous ou-blie, Pois-sons de la mé-lan-co-lie.

Pont sur Seine
Avril, Mai 1919

Sarabande

René Chalupt
(1885-1957)

Albert Roussel
(1869-1937)

Composed 1919. Opus 20: *Deux mélodies*, no. 2. Published by Durand. Dedicated to Madame Lucy Vuillemin. "Sarabande," perhaps Roussel's most beautiful mélodie, is an outstanding example of his evocative pianistic writing and expressive musical imagery. Chalupt's poetry, with its discreet but voluptuous imagery, seemed to fit Roussel's elegant and restrained temperament well, and inspired some of the composer's best mélodies. There is an oriental delicacy in Roussel's evocation of the fluttering doves, feathers into a pool, and the slow drift of chestnut blossoms onto bare flesh. Chalupt's dancing fountains are direct descendants of Verlaine's jets d'eau in "Clair de lune" (see Fauré's setting), but in this context are more intimate and mysterious. Chalupt and Roussel were close friends; Roussel composed two sets of songs to Chalupt poetry (Opus 20 and Opus 50). For Roussel's sixtieth birthday celebration Chalupt wrote a poem about Roussel ("La marin favorisé") which composer Maurice Delage set to music as part of a special tribute concert.

Sarabande	*Saraband*
Les jet d'eau dansent des sarabandes	*The fountains are dancing sarabands*
Sur l'herbe parfumée des boulingrins;	*On the fragrant grass of the lawns;*
Il y a des rumeurs de soie dans le jardin	*There are sounds of rustling silk in the garden*
Et de mystérieuses présences.	*And mysterious presences.*
Sur le marbre rose d'une margelle,	*On the rim of a pink marble fountain,*
Trois tourterelles se sont posées,	*Three turtle-doves have lighted,*
Comme sur tes lèvres trois baisers;	*Like three kisses on your lips;*
Leurs plumes s'éffeuillent dans le bassin.	*Their feathers fall like leaves into the basin.*
Les fleurs fraîches des marronniers	*The fresh flowers of the chestnut trees*
Neigent lentement sur tes seins	*Fall slowly like snowflakes on your breast*
Et font frissonner ta chair nue,	*Making your bare flesh shiver,*
Car tu es nue sous ton manteau.	*For you are naked under your cloak.*
Et c'est pour toi que les jets d'eau	*And it is for you that the fountains*
Dansent de sveltes sarabandes,	*Dance their slender sarabands*
Que le parc est plein de présences,	*That the park is full of presences,*
Et que les tourterelles blanches,	*And that the white turtle-doves,*
Comme de vivantes guirlandes,	*Like living garlands,*
Viennent fleurir au bord de l'eau.	*Come to flower at the water's edge.*

dan - sent des sa - ra - ban - des

Sur l'her - be par - fu -

mé - e des bou - lin - grins; _____

Il y a des ru-meurs de soie _____ dans le jar - din _____ Et _____

_____ de mys - té - ri - eu - ses pré - sen - ces.

Le bachelier de Salamanque

René Chalupt
(1885-1957)

Albert Roussel
(1869-1937)

Composed 1919. Opus 20: *Deux mélodies*, no. 1. Publisher: Durand. Dedicated to Jacques Durand. First performance by Mme. Lucy Vuillemin, Paris, 27 December, 1919. "Le bachelier de Salamanque" provides a comic contrast to "Sarabande," the other mélodie of Opus 20. Chalupt's poem describes quite a different serenader from those found in Verlaine's elegant manicured gardens (see "Mandoline"). This hero is a university student, determined to deliver his musical offering after curfew has rung. His furtive journey through the streets of Salamanca is accompanied by a lively pastiche of Spanish music. Roussel trained as a naval officer until 1894, when he left his maritime career to devote himself entirely to music. He studied and eventually taught at the Schola Cantorum, established by César Franck's disciple Vincent d'Indy. Satie and Varèse were among Roussel's students. He always retained his love for the sea, describing his musical works as attempts to "evoke all the feelings which lie hidden in the sea—the sense of power and infinity, of charm, anger and gentleness . . . " One of the most well-traveled of composers, Roussel was always drawn to exotic destinations, notably the Orient. The living room of the "sailor-musician" was painted a dark blue in order to show to advantage the beauty of his golden Indian statues.

Le bachelier de Salamanque	The Student from Salamanca
Où vas-tu, toi qui passes si tard	*Where are you going, you who pass so late*
Dans les rues désertes de Salamanque,	*In the deserted streets of Salamanca,*
Avec ta toque noire et ta guitare,	*With your black cap and guitar,*
Que tu dissimules sous ta mante?	*Hidden beneath your cloak?*
Le couvre-feu est déjà sonné	*The curfew has already sounded*
Et depuis longtemps dans leurs paisibles maisons	*And for hours in their peaceful homes*
Les bourgeois dorment à poings fermés.	*The burghers have been sound asleep.*
Ne sais-tu pas qu'un édit de l'alcade	*Do you not know the alcade has decreed*
Ordonne de jeter en prison	*Prison as punishment for those*
Tous les donneurs de sérénade,	*Who sing their serenades,*
Que les malandrins couperont ta chaîne d'or,	*That brigands will cut your golden chain,*
Et que la fille de l'Almirante,	*And that the Admiral's daughter*
Pour qui vainement tu te tourmentes,	*For whom you sigh in vain*
Se moque de toi, derrière son mirador?	*Mocks you from her mirador?*

alcade: sheriff
Almirante: Admiral, commander of a fleet
mirador: an enclosed balcony with a shuttered window

Un peu moins animé

pp

Le cou - vre - feu est dé - jà son -

né _____ Et de - puis long -

temps dans leurs pai - si - bles mai - sons _____

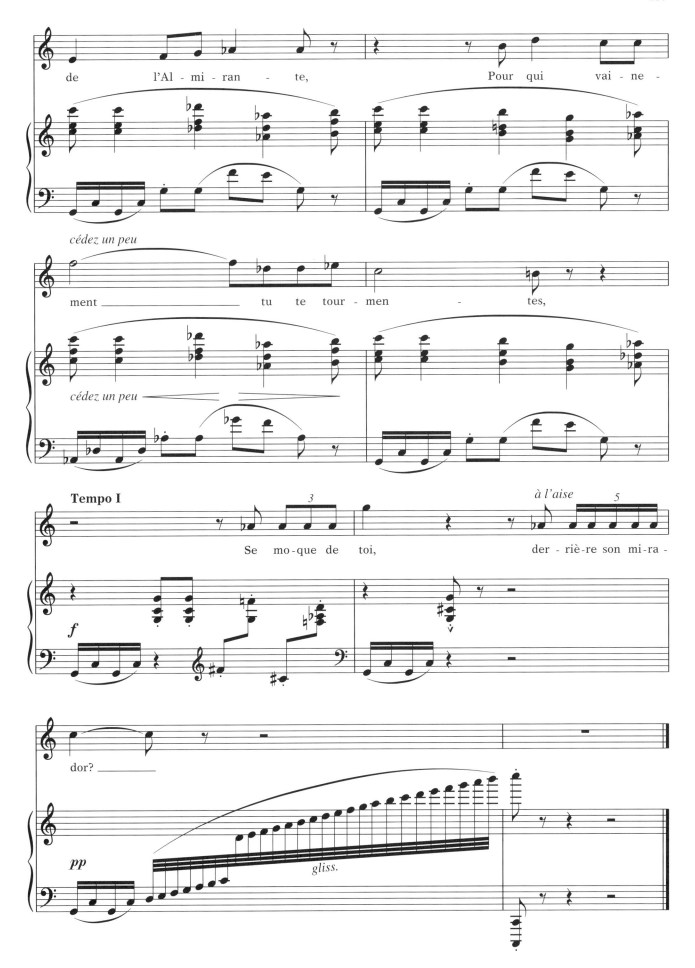

de l'Al - mi - ran - te, Pour qui vai - ne -

cédez un peu

ment _____ tu te tour - men - tes,

cédez un peu

Tempo I

Se mo - que de toi,

à l'aise

der - riè - re son mi - ra -

dor? _____

pp

gliss.

Sainte

Stéphane Mallarmé
(1842-1898)

Maurice Ravel
(1875-1938)

Composed 1896. Published by Durand, 1907. Dedicated to Madame Edmond Bonniot, Mallarmé's daughter. "Sainte" was Ravel's first published song. He kept the manuscript in his private folio from 1896 to 1907, when he finally agreed to have it published by Durand. Mallarmé dedicated his poem to St. Cecilia, the patron saint of musicians, describing it as "a little song-like poem written above all with music in mind." The words have a mystical, chant-like quality that evokes the church's hushed atmosphere and the unheard melodies issuing from the stained glass window. In the poem's final lines, Mallarmé captures the stillness of the stained glass itself. Ravel considered Mallarmé the greatest of French poets, and used his verses nineteen years later for a work for voice and chamber orchestra, *Trois poèmes de Mallarmé*.

Sainte	Saint
À la fenêtre recélant	*At the recessed window*
Le santal vieux qui se dédore	*The old fading sandalwood*
De sa viole étincelant	*Of her viol that sparkled*
Jadis selon* flûte ou mandore,	*Once to flute or mandola,*
Est la Sainte pâle, étalant	*Is the pale Saint, displaying*
Le livre vieux qui se déplie	*The old book that lies open*
Du Magnificat ruisselant	*To the Magnificat that glistened*
Jadis selon vêpres et** complie:	*Once to vespers and compline:*
À ce vitrage d'ostensoir	*At this glass monstrance*
Que frôle un harpe par l'Ange	*Brushed by an angel's harp*
Formée avec son vol du soir	*Formed with his evening flight*
Pour la délicate phalange	*For the delicate point*
Du doigt que, san le vieux santal,	*Of the finger that, without the old sandalwood*
Ni le vieux libre, elle balance	*And the ancient book, she poises*
Sur le plumage instrumental,	*On the instrumental plumage,*
Musicienne du silence.	*Musician of silence.*

*Mallarmé's original word here is "avec" rather than "selon" (changed by Ravel)
**Mallarmé's original word here is "et" rather than "ou" (changed by Ravel)

À ce vi - tra - ge d'os - ten -

soir Que frôle u - ne har - pe par l'An - ge For - mée a - vec son vol du

soir _____ Pour la dé - li - ca - te pha - lan -

Cinq mélodies populaires grecques

Traditional Greek folk songs
Translated into French by M.D. Calvocoressi

Maurice Ravel
(1875-1938)

Le réveil de la mariée
Là-bas, vers l'église
Quel galant m'est comparable?
Chanson des cueilleuses de lentisques
Tout gai!

Composed 1904. Original texts in Greek. Published by Durand in 1906 in Calvocoressi's French translations. First performance by Marguerite Babaïan. Ravel later began orchestrating the collection, but lost interest after completing the first and last songs. Manuel Rosenthal, Ravel's friend and disciple, completed scoring the remaining three songs in 1935. There is also a version for harp and voice.

Ravel composed the accompaniments in 1904. French musicologist Pierre Aubry needed musical examples to illustrate a lecture he was giving on Greek folk song. M.D. Calvocoressi, a friend of Greek descent, selected five songs and taught them phonetically to Louise Thomasset, who was to sing the examples during the lecture. She insisted on having piano accompaniment, so Aubry turned to Ravel, who composed the accompaniments in 36 hours. Two of the five songs performed, "Quel galant m'est comparable?" and "Chanson des cueilleuses de lentisques," were later incorporated into the *Cinq mélodies populaires grecques*. Three of the songs subsequently vanished, but Ravel later set three other mélodies chosen by Calvocoressi and these complete the collection as it is performed today.

These five genuine Greek folk songs are based on Greek dance rhythms. Ravel's settings might be described as "neo-Hellenic" for their clarity in line and structure, qualities that enhance the poetic and melodic material. The songs capture colorful animated scenes from Greek peasant life. Ravel seemed to relish working with folk song. In 1910, he created imaginative settings for a collection of Spanish, French, Italian and Hebrew melodies (*Chants populaires*) and in 1914 set *Deux mélodies hébraïques*.

Le réveil de la mariée

Le réveil de la mariée

Réveille-toi, réveille-toi, perdris mignonne.
Ouvre au matin tes ailes.
Trois grains de beauté, mon cœur en est brûle.
Vois le ruban, le ruban d'or que je t'apporte
Pour le nouer autour de tes cheveux.
Si tu veux, ma belle, viens nous marier:
Dans nos deux familles, tous sont alliés.

The bride's awakening

Wake up, wake up, pretty partridge.
Open your wings to the morning.
Three beauty spots have set my heart on fire.
See the ribbon, the golden ribbon I bring you
To tie round your hair.
If you want, my beauty, come let's be married:
In our two families, all are kindred.

toi, per - drix mi - gnon - ne. Ouvre au ma -

tin tes ai - les,

ouvre ___ au ma - tin tes ai -

les. Trois grains de beau - té, mon

cœur en est brû - lé. Trois grains de beau -

té, mon cœur en est brû - lé.

Vois le ru -

ban, le ru - ban d'or que je t'ap - por - te,

vois le ru - ban, le ru - ban d'or que je t'ap -

por - te Pour le nou - er au -

tour de tes che - veux, _____ pour ___ le nou -

er au - tour de tes che - veux.

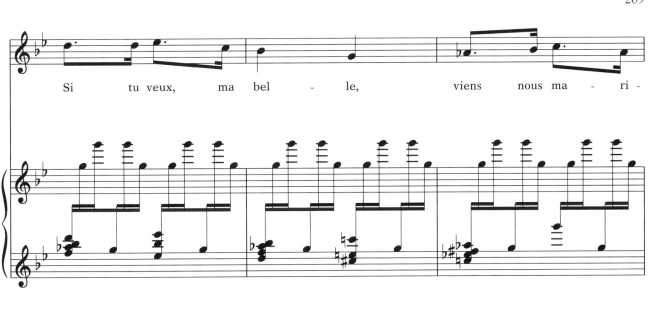

Si tu veux, ma bel - le, viens nous ma - ri -

rall. poco a poco

er: Dans nos deux fa - mil - les,

tous sont al - li - és.

La-bàs, vers l'église

La-bàs, vers l'église

La-bàs, vers l'église	*Over there, near the church*
Vers l'église Ayio Sidero,	*Near the church of Saint Sideros*
L'église, ô Vierge sainte,	*The church, O Holy Virgin,*
L'église, Ayio Costanndino	*The church of Saint Constantine*
Se sont réunis, rassemblés en nombre infini,	*They are gathered, assembled in inifinite number,*
Du monde, ô Vierge sainte!	*In the world, O Holy Virgin*
Du monde tous les plus braves!	*All the bravest in the world!*

271

Quel galant m'est comparable?

Quel galant m'est comparable?   *What gallant can compare with me?*

Quel galant m'est comparable,   *What gallant can compare with me?*
D'entre ceux qu'on voit passer?   *Among those seen passing by?*
Dis, Dame Vassiliki?   *Tell me, Lady Vassiliki?*
Vois, pendus, pendus à ma ceinture,   *See, hung on my belt,*
Pistolets et sabre aigu…   *Pistols and a sharp sword…*
Et c'est toi que j'aime!   *And it is you whom I love!*

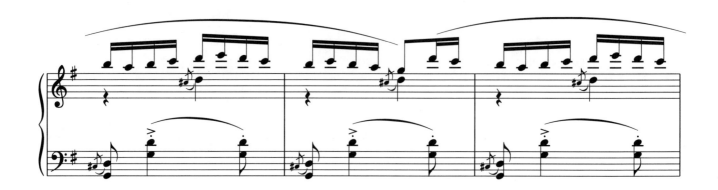

Chanson des cueilleuses de lentisques

Chanson des cueilleuses de lentisques

Ô joie de mon âme,
Joie de mon cœur, trésor qui m'est si cher;
Joie de l'âme et du cœur.

Toi que j'aime ardemment,
Tu es plus beau qu'un ange.
Ô lorsque tu parais, ange si doux,
Devant nos yeux,
Comme un bel ange blond,
Sous le clair soleil,
Hélas, tous nos pauvres cœurs soupirent!

Song of the lentisk gatherers

O joy of my soul,
Joy of my heart, treasure so dear to me;
Joy of the soul and of the heart.

You whom I love passionately
You are lovelier than an angel
O when you appear, angel so sweet
Before our eyes,
Like a beautiful blonde angel,
In the bright sunlight
Alas! all our poor hearts sigh!

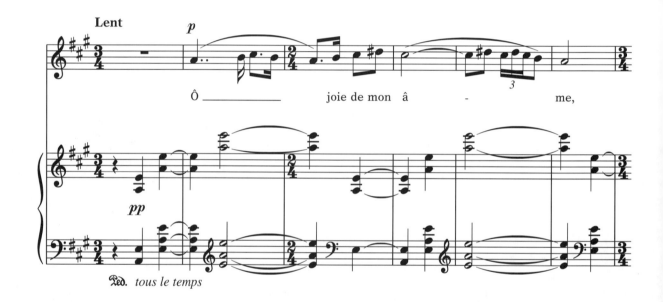

Joie de l'âme et _ du cœur. _ Toi que j'aime ar - dem - ment, _

Tu es plus beau, plus beau qu'un _ an - ge. ____

Ô _____ lors-que tu pa - rais, an - ge _ si

doux, _____ an - ge si _ doux, De -vant nos _

yeux, _____

Comme un bel an - ge blond, Sous le clair so - leil, ___

Hé - las, tous nos _____ pau-vres cœurs sou -

pi - rent!

Tout gai!

Tout gai!	All merry!
Tout gai,	All merry,
Ha, tout gai;	Ha! all merry;
Belle jambe, tireli qui danse,	Beautiful legs, tireli that dance,
Belle jambe, la vaisselle danse,	Beautiful legs, the pottery dances,
Tra-la-la.	Tra-la-la.

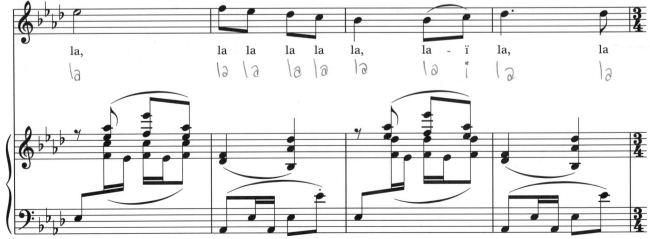

Aimons-nous

Théodore de Banville
(1823-1891)

Camille Saint-Saëns
(1835-1921)

Composed 1881. Théodore de Banville's poem has no title, but is from *Les Exilés*, Odelettes (1878). Poet, playwright and novelist, Banville produced some twenty collections of verse and was highly regarded by the younger poets of his day. Saint-Saëns dedicated this mélodie to Paul Vidal. The composer had a keen sense of public taste, and no doubt created "Aimons-nous" to appeal to the music consumers of the day. Its highly sentimental setting is somewhat reminiscent of Massenet's "Elégie." Both songs were great hits with the public and are still among the most popular mélodies of both composers.

Aimons-nous	*Let us love*
Aimons-nous et dormons	*Let us love and sleep*
San songer au reste du monde!	*Without dreaming of the rest of the world!*
Ni le flot de la mer, ni l'ouragan des monts	*Neither the ocean waves, nor the mountain storm*
Tant que nous nous aimons	*For as long as we love each other,*
Ne courbera ta tête blonde,	*Will trouble your golden head,*
Car l'amour est plus fort	*For love is stronger*
Que les Dieux et la Mort!	*Than the Gods and Death!*
Le soleil s'éteindrait	*The sun would cease to burn*
Pour laisser ta blancheur plus pure,	*To make your purity more pure,*
Le vent qui jusqu'à terre incline la forêt,	*The wind that bends even the forest to the ground,*
En passant n'oserait	*Would not dare in passing*
Jouer avec ta chevelure,	*To play with your tresses*
Tant que tu chaceras	*So long as you hide*
Ta tête entre mes bras!	*Your head in my arms!*
Et lorsque nos deux cœurs	*And when our two hearts*
S'en iront aux sphères heureuses	*Shall soar into blissful realms*
Où les célestes lys écloront sous nos pleurs,	*Where heavenly lilies open beneath our tears,*
Alors, comme deux fleurs,	*Then, like two flowers,*
Joignons nos lèvres amoureuses,	*Let us join our loving lips,*
Et tâchons d'épuiser	*And try to outlast*
La mort dans un baiser!	*Death with a kiss!*

Dieux et la Mort!

Le so - leil s'ét -tein - drait Pour lais-

ser ta blan -cheur plus pu - re, Le vent qui jus-qu'à terre in-cli-ne la fo-rêt,

En pas -sant n'o-se - rait Jou-er a-vec ta che-ve - lu - re,

Et lors-que nos deux cœurs S'en i - ront aux sphè-res heu - reu - ses

sempre **pp**

Où les cé-les-tes lys é-clo-ront sous nos pleurs, A - lors, com - me deux

poco cresc.

rit. *dim.* *a tempo* **pp**

fleurs, __ Joi-gnons nos lèv-res a-mou-reu - ses,

p
rit.

pp
a tempo

L'attente

Victor Hugo
(1802-1885)

Camille Saint-Saëns
(1835-1921)

Composed 1851. The text is found in Victor Hugo's *Les Orientales* (1828), no. 20. Saint-Saëns was a child prodigy—his earliest extant manuscript was composed at age four! His talent was far ranging—composer, pianist, organist, writer. He served as the organist at the Madeleine in Paris; Liszt declared him to be the greatest organist in the world. Berlioz's description of Saint-Saëns was somewhat sharper: "He knows everything, but lacks inexperience." Saint-Saëns composed more than 100 mélodies; the best of them display his spontaneous lyrical gift and skilled craftsmanship. Richard Wagner, who titled his mélodie "Attente", also set Hugo's dramatic poem. It is possible that the twenty-year-old Saint-Saëns, who much admired Wagner, modeled his song on Wagner's setting.

L'attente

Monte, écureuil, monte au grand chêne,
Sur la branche des cieux prochaine,
Qui plie et tremble comme un jonc.
Cigogne, aux vieilles tours fidèle,
Oh! vole et monte à tire-d'aile
De l'église à la citadelle,
Du haut clocher au grand donjon.

Vieux aigle, monte de ton aire
À la montagne centenaire
Que blanchit l'hiver éternel.
Et toi qu'en ta couche inquiète
Jamais l'aube ne vit muette,
Monte, monte, vive alouette,
Vive alouette, monte au ciel!

Et maintenant, du haut de l'arbre,
Des flèches de la tour de marbre
Du grand mont, du ciel enflammé,
A l'horizon, parmi la brume,
Voyez-vous flotter une plume,
Et courir un cheval qui fume,
Et revenir ma bien-aimée?

Waiting

Climb, squirrel, climb the great oak,
To the branch nearest the sky,
That bends and trembles like a reed.
Stork, inhabitant of ancient towers,
Oh! Swiftly fly and wing your way
From the church to the fortress,
From the high steeple to the mighty keep.

Old eagle, rise from your eyrie
To the ancient mountain peak
Eternally white with snow.
And you, ever restless in your nest
Who never fails to greet the dawn,
Rise, rise, lively lark,
Ascend into the sky!

And now from the high tree-top,
From the marble tower's spire,
From the mountain crest, from the flaming sky,
On the horizon, in the mist,
Do you see a fluttering plume
And a steaming, galloping horse
And my beloved returning home?

chai - ne, Qui plie et trem - ble comme un jonc.

marcato

cresc.

Ci-gogne, aux vie-illes tours fi - dè - le, Oh!

f

fp

vole et monte à ti - re - d'ai - le De l'é -

glise à la ci-ta-del - le, Du haut clo-cher au grand don-jon.

marcato

A l'ho - ri - zon, _____ par - mi la bru - me, Voy - ez

vous flot - ter _____ u - ne plu - me, Et cou -

rir un che - val qui fu - me, Et re - ve - nir ma bien - ai

mée, et _____ re - ve - nir _____

Je te veux

Henry Pacory

Erik Satie
(1866-1925)

"Valse chantée ," composed 1897. For voice and piano, originally written for tenor voice. First published by Baudoux, 1902; Bellon Ponscarme, 1903; Rouart-Lerolle. Version for solo piano, Bellon Ponscarme, 1904. The popular song was subsequently published in a number of instrumental versions. In Paris at the turn of the century, café concerts (caf'conç) and the music-halls were the entertainments of choice for the working class. These reflected the glamour and gaiety of the City of Light, and offered a stimulating atmosphere in which to unwind. It was a lean time for Satie, who was barely able to eke out a living writing pot-boilers for the caf'conç and singers like Paulette Darty, its reigning star. A statuesque blonde with an ample figure and a stage presence that commanded the attention of the most boisterous Saturday night audience, Darty was billed as the "Queen of the *Valse Chantée*;" in between the verses and at the end of every song, she waltzed around the stage in graceful circles. The *valse chantée* was staple musical fare of the caf'conç, sentimental and tuneful, usually with racy lyrics. Satie met Darty in 1903 when he auditioned "Je te veux" for her: "In the mornings I was in the habit of receiving composers who brought me new songs. . . I was resting when. . .suddenly, I heard the now famous waltz 'Je te veux'. . . It had such a special charm. . . that I slipped into a peignoir to go and express my delight to Monsieur Satie. He went back to the piano, and I sang 'Je te veux' for the first time." Darty immediately added it to her repertoire and its popularity was assured. Lyricist Henry Pacory was a close friend of Satie's who usually paid the composer's tab at the caf'conc's. Before the song was published, Pacory's rather explicit poem was watered down at Satie's request. Manuscript revisions in Satie's handwriting suggest he may have taken part in changing some of the text himself.

Je te veux	*I want you*
J'ai compris ta détresse,	*I've understood your distress*
Cher amoureux.	*Dear lover.*
Et je cède à te vœux:	*And I yield to your desires:*
Fais de moi ta maîtresse.	*Make me your mistress.*
Loin de nous la sagesse,	*Let's throw discretion away*
Plus de détresse,	*No more sadness,*
J'aspire à l'instant précieux	*I long for the precious moment*
Où nous serons heureux:	*When we will be happy:*
Je te veux.	*I want you.*
Je n'ai pas de regrets,	*I have no regrets,*
Et je n'ai qu'une envie:	*And only one desire:*
Près de toi, là, tout près,	*Close to you, there, very close,*
Vivre toute ma vie.	*To live my whole life.*
Que mon cœur soit le tien	*Let my heart be yours*
Et ta lèvre la mienne,	*And your lips mine*
Que ton corps soit le mien,	*Let your body be mine*
Et que toute ma chair soit tienne.	*And all my flesh yours.*
J'ai compris ta détresse. . .	*I've understood your distress. . .*
Oui, je vois dans tes yeux	*Yes, I see in your eyes*
Le divine promesse	*The divine promise*
Que ton coeur amoureux	*That your loving heart*
Vient chercher ma caresse.	*Is seeking my caress.*
Enlacés pour toujours,	*Forever entwined together*
Brûlés des mêmes flammes,	*Seared by the same desire*
Dans des rêves d'amours,	*In dreams of love*
Nous échangerons nos deux âmes.	*We'll exchange our two souls.*

moi ta _____ maî - tres - se. Loin de nous la sa -

ges - se, Plus de tris - tes - se, J'as -

pire à l'ins - tant pré - ci - eux Où nous se - rons heu - reux: _____ Je te

Premier
COUPLET

veux. _____ Je n'ai *p* pas _____ de re - grets, _____ Et je

n'ai qu'u - ne en - vi - e: Près de toi, _____ là, tout

près, _____ Vi - vre tou - te _____ ma vi - e. Que mon

cœur _____ soit le tien _____ Et ta lè - vre _____ la

mien - ne, Que ton corps _____ soit le mien, _____ Et que

La statue de bronze

Léon-Paul Fargue
(1876-1947)

Erik Satie
(1866-1925)

Composed 1916. First song in published order, *Trois mélodies de 1916* but composed last. Publisher: Rouart-Lerolle, 1917; Salabert. Orchestrated by Robert Caby, Salabert, 1968. Dedicated to Jane Bathori, who premiered the first two songs of the set, "Daphénéo" and "Le Chapelier," in April of 1916 with pianist Ricardo Viñes. In May 1916, Bathori and Satie performed all three songs in a concert presented in connection with an exhibition of modern painting. The program for this recital featured original engravings by Matisse and Picasso. This song was Satie's first setting of the poetry of Léon-Paul Fargue, the "Bohemian poet of Paris." Satie used Fargue's witty verses again for *Ludions* (1923), a kaleidoscopic cycle of musical miniatures. "La statue de bronze" can be linked to "La grenouille Américaine" (The American frog) found in *Ludions*. Both songs share accompaniment figures spun-off from the music hall style. "La statue de bronze" is both ironic and wistful. It is quintessential Satie—brief, laconic, and witty. Francis Poulenc referred to this song as strongly influencing his melodic style: "I cherish it with a secret fondness and endless gratitude. "

La statue de bronze	*The bronze statue*
La grenouille du jeu de tonneau*	*The frog of the game of tonneau*
S'ennuie, le soir, sous la tonnelle…	*Gets bored, at evening under the arbor.*
Elle en a assez!	*She has had enough!*
D'être la statue	*Of being a statue*
Qui va prononcer un grand mot, le Mot!	*About to pronounce an important word, the Word!*
Elle aimerait mieux être avec les autres	*She would rather be with the others*
Qui font des bulles de musique	*Blowing music bubbles*
Avec le savon de la lune	*With the soap of the moon.*
Au bord du lavoir mordoré	*At the edge of the reddish-brown washhouse*
Qu'on voit, là-bas, luire entre les branches…	*Shining over there between the branches…*
On lui lance à cœur de journée	*All day long they keep throwing*
Une pâture de pistols	*Fodder of metal disks*
Qui la traversent sans lui profiter	*That only pass through her*
Et s'en vont sonner	*And go rattling*
Dans les cabinets	*Into the compartments*
De son piédestal numéroté!	*Of her numbered pedestal!*
Et le soir les insectes couchent	*And at night, the insects sleep*
Dans sa bouche.	*In her mouth.*

*The "jeu de tonneau" was a garden game popular at the end of the 19th century. The goal of the game was to throw metal discs through the frog's mouth into numbered compartments that determined the player's score.

Pas trop vite

La gre-nouil-le du jeu de ton-neau S'en-nui-e, le soir, sous la ton-nel - le... Elle en a as-sez! D'ê-tre la sta-tu - e Qui va pro-non - cer un grand mot, le Mot!

Les hiboux

Charles Baudelaire
(1821-1867)

Déodat de Sévérac
(1872-1921)

Composed 1898. Published by Rouart, Lerolle, 1913. Déodat de Sévérac was born in the Languedoc region of southwest France. After his studies in Paris, he returned home and remained there, traveling to Paris only when necessary. He attended the Schola Cantorum, studying with Magnard and d'Indy. He composed piano and orchestra music, songs and operas. His family, childhood, and the culture of his native Languedoc figured prominently in his music; he often wrote parts for regional folk instruments in his scores. He often referred to himself as "the peasant musician." His music shows influences of Debussy, Mussorgsky, and in his early songs, Bizet. "Les hiboux" is considered one of his best songs, depicting the hollow sound of the owls' call effectively in the piano writing.

Les hiboux

Sous les ifs noirs qui les abritent,
Les hiboux se tiennent rangés,
Ainsi que des Dieux étrangers;
Dardant leur œil rouge ils méditent.

Sans remuer ils se tiendront
Jusqu'a l'heure mélancolique
Où, poussant le soleil oblique,
Les ténèbres s'établiront.

Leur attitude au sage enseigne
Qu'il faut en ce monde qu'il craigne
Le tumulte et le mouvement;

L'homme ivre d'une ombre qui passe
Porte toujours le châtiment
D'avoir voulu changer de place!

Owls

Beneath the shelter of the black yew-trees
The owls perch in a row
Like strange gods, whose
Red eyes gleam, they meditate.

They will remain motionless
Until the melancholy hour
When, pushing aside the slanting sun
The shadows establish themselves.

From their attitude the wise man learns
That in the world he should fear
All movement and disturbance;

The man intoxicated with passing shadows
Always pays a penalty
For choosing to roam.

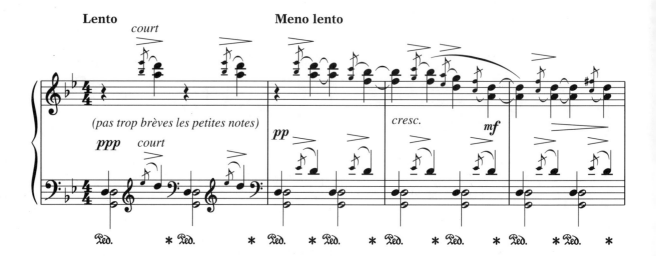

Sous les ifs noirs qui les a-
bri - tent, Les hi-boux se tien - nent ran - gés, Ain-si que des
Dieux é-tran-gers; Dar-dant leur œil rou - ge ils mé-di -

nè - bres _____ s'é - ta - bli - ront.

Leur at - ti - tude   au sage en - sei - gne Qu'il faut   en ce mon - de qu'il

crai - gne le tu - mul - te   Et   le mou - ve - ment; _____

Meno lento

310

Philis

Anonymous
Rondeau chanté, d'après un manuscrit du XVIIe siècle

Déodat de Sévérac
(1872-1921)

Composed 1916. *Douze mélodies*, Published by Rouart-Lerolle. This is the last song in the set. Sévérac's subtitle indicates the lineage of the poem as 18th century. Perhaps, perhaps not— in any case, Sévérac's fresh setting has the musical veneer of an earlier century (see also Hahn's "À Chloris"). This delightful pastiche was part of a group of songs Sévérac arranged for Yvette Guilbert (1868-1944), a Parisian actress and *diseuse* who performed in the café-concerts. She was the subject of a number of cariacatures and drawings by Toulouse-Lautrec.

Philis

Par un souris l'Amour surpris
Malgré Psyché vous rend les armes;
Bacchus auprès de vos attraits
D'Ariane brave les charmes.

Chacun d'eux osa prétendre
Un favorable succès;
Pour vous rendre le cœur tendre
Ils vous offrent tout exprès
L'un son verre, l'autre ses traits.

De cette double victoire
Vos appas étaient garants
Mais Philis, daignez m'en croire,
Préférez à de tels amants
Un mortel qui vous adore
Mille fois plus qu'eux encore.
Ô Philis!

Phyllis

Cupid, surprised by your smile
Despite Psyche, surrenders his weapons to you;
Confronted with your allure, Bacchus
Braves Ariadne's charms.

Both Cupid and Bacchus dared
Claim a favorable success;
To soften your heart,
They instantly offer you
One his glass, the other his arrows.

This double victory
Was guaranteed by your charms
But Philis, pray believe me,
And prefer over such lovers
A mortal who adores you
A thousand times more than they.
Oh, Phyllis!

2ᵉ Couplet
Un peu lent

bra - ve les char - mes. ___ De cet - te dou - ble vic -

toi - re Vos ap - pas é - taient ga - rants Mais Phi -

lis, dai - gnez m'en croi - re, ___ Pré - fé - rez à de tels a -

mants Un mor - tel qui vous a - do - re ___ Mil - le

Fleur desséchée

Alexandre Pushkin
(1799-1837)
Translated from the Russian by Louis Pomey

Pauline Viardot
(1821-1910)

Autograph not traced. Song no. 1 in *Douze mélodies sur des poésies russes*, published by Gérard, 1866. Pauline Viardot, a woman of extraordinary talent and intelligence, was an important figure in the artistic activities of her time. An illustrious singer from a legendary musical family, she became an inspirational catalyst for many composers. She studied piano with Liszt; Saint-Saëns and Chopin often accompanied her at the piano. She inspired operas: Meyerbeer composed the role of Fidès in *Le prophète* (1849) for her, and in 1851 Gounod wrote *Sapho* for her. Her most celebrated role was Orphée in Berlioz's French version of Gluck's *Orfeo ed Euridice*; she sang the role over 150 times in a single year. Her daughter, Marianne, was for a time engaged to Gabriel Fauré (see "Après un rêve"). Clara Schumann said of her: "Viardot is the most gifted woman I have ever met in my life." Pauline Viardot composed over 100 songs, more than 90 were published during her lifetime.

Fleur desséchée	*Pressed flower*
Dans ce vieux livre l'on t'oublie,	*In this old book you have been forgotten*
Fleur sans parfum et sans couleur,	*Flower without scent or color*
Mais une étrange rêverie,	*But a strange reverie*
Quand je te vois, emplit mon cœur.	*Fills my heart when I see you.*
Quel jour, quel lieu te virent naître?	*What day, what place witnessed your birth?*
Quel fut ton sort? qui t'arracha?	*What was your destiny? Who picked you?*
Qui sait? Je les connus peut-être,	*Who knows? Perhaps I knew*
Ceux dont l'amour te conserva!	*Those whose love preserved you!*
Rappelais-tu, rose flétrie,	*Faded rose, do you recall*
La première heure ou les adieux?	*The first hours or the farewells?*
Les entretiens dans la prairie	*The conversations in the meadow*
Ou dans le bois silencieux?	*Or in the silent wood?*
Vit-il encor? existe-t-elle?	*Is he still living? Does she exist?*
À quels rameaux flottent leurs nids!	*On which branches do their nests sway?*
Ou comme toi, qui fus si belle,	*Or like you, who were so lovely,*
Leurs fronts charmants sont-ils flétris?	*Are their charming looks withered?*

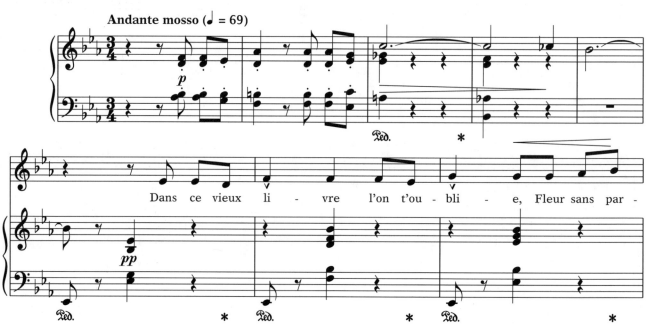

Animato

Quel jour, quel lieu te vi - rent

naî - tre? Quel fut _____ ton

sort? qui t'ar - ra - cha? Qui sait? Je

les con - nus peut - ê - tre, Ceux dont l'a -